SEARCHING FOR JANE CROW

BLACK WOMEN AND MASS INCARCERATION IN AMERICA FROM THE AUCTION BLOCK TO THE CELL BLOCK

TALITHA L. LEFLOURIA

BEACON PRESS, BOSTON

BEACON PRESS
24 Farnsworth Street
Boston, Massachusetts
www.beacon.org

Beacon Press books
are published under the auspices of
the Unitarian Universalist Association of Congregations.

29 28 27 26 8 7 6 5 4 3 2 1

This book is printed on acid-free paper that meets the uncoated paper ANSI/NISO specifications for permanence as revised in 1992.

Text design and composition by Kim Arney

Library of Congress Cataloguing-in-Publication Data is available for this title.
Hardcover ISBN: 978-0-8070-0393-0
E-book ISBN: 978-0-8070-0394-7
Audiobook: 978-0-8070-0383-1

The authorized representative in the EU for product safety and compliance is Easy Access System Europe 16879218, Mustamäe tee 50, 10621 Tallinn, Estonia: https://beacon.org/eu-contact.

For the women

CONTENTS

AUTHOR'S NOTE

On July 31, 2024, I visited the Orleans Justice Center in New Orleans, Louisiana. I entered the pod, which resembled an oversized cage with heavy iron doors and small rooms filled with women's unrealized dreams and hidden potential. Although I was only visiting, I could not help feeling fearful of becoming trapped on the inside. However, my anxiety disappeared when I saw the women.

Light filled their eyes as they emerged from their cramped cells into the spacious common area—they were undoubtedly happy to have a break from confinement. They clung to the moment as they would the paper with their public defender's phone number or a valuable personal belonging.

I began giving the women a history lesson about mass incarceration and its effects on Black women in the past. Most of the women in jail that day were Black, and they empathized with the plight of enslaved and free Black women who found themselves on the wrong side of the law—incarcerated for no reason other than their Black skin.

Sharing the history lesson was easy, but when I was asked about my own story, I felt afraid. As I looked out at the women, all in matching burgundy scrubs and orange rubber slides, I could not help but envision the possibilities for their futures—and for my own, had my mistakes carried me on a different path. I felt courage fill my soul, and I began telling my story, a story I am sharing publicly for the first time.

Like most seven-year-old girls, I enjoyed playing dress-up and make-believe. Sometimes I was a princess, and other times, I was a teacher. However, all the time, I was hurting.

Three months before my eighth birthday, my father died suddenly and violently. I won't share the details of his death out of respect for my family's privacy, but the circumstances became my secret shame. I buried it deep within me, in the areas left untouched by my grief. However, it grew over time and eventually revealed itself through a near-fatal overdose.

I had never considered myself a trauma survivor, or a person with adverse childhood experiences, until I met a community of formerly incarcerated women who changed my life. They helped me put my lived experience into perspective and modeled bravery by sharing their stories, making me eventually feel comfortable enough to share mine.

I grew up in a working-class family in a poor community. We were what some would call "hood rich." My mother drove a Cadillac, we shopped at JCPenney, and we were well provided for; she often prided herself on the fact that we were two hundred dollars above the income requirement to qualify for free lunch.

My mother sent us to school with food purchased from her wages as a supervisor of housekeeping at a local hospital. We walked about a mile every morning to school; our severely underfunded district could not afford a bus for us. And as it did in many Black communities in America during the mid-1980s, the War on Drugs ripped through our small town of Ypsilanti, Michigan. Some of my classmates lost their mothers and fathers to prison, leaving them in the care of relatives or the state. I empathized with them, understanding the profound pain of being separated from family.

In the final months of my father's life, my family scattered like puzzle pieces. I lived with my great-aunt while my mother and brothers lived up the street. My father lived alone. It felt strange to be separated, but the conditions in our household had become overwhelming. My father was a loving man and my favorite person in the world, but he also had a temper.

By the time I reached the third grade, I had cycled through three different elementary schools. I remember them all, as well as my teachers. But the one I remember most vividly nearly changed the course of my educational career. My parent-teacher conferences always ended in the same way, with my mother telling me to stop talking so much and being disruptive in class. She knew I was bored so she asked my teachers to give me more challenging assignments, but few listened. However, it was my "inability to share" with other students in my second-grade class—an offense I still cannot understand—that got me placed in the "Learning Center," or what we referred to in the 1980s as special ed.

Mrs. Mitchell, a Black woman who worked as a classroom aide, looked after me every day. *I absolutely adored her*. She eventually saved me from this institutionalized learning environment where we were taught very little and ostracized from the general student population. I remember her making a fuss with whoever would listen at the school, insisting that I did not belong there. None of us did. The Learning Center was, in effect, a detention setting for children who learned differently (the school population was around 80 percent Black).

By the spring of 1986, I moved home and rejoined my family. I was so happy to be able to play with my brothers, make new friends, and enjoy my childhood. Then my father died tragically.

I did not have any vocabulary to express how I felt inside, but I knew it was unusual. It was a pain I had never experienced before, in a place I could not soothe. This was greater than a scraped knee. How would I navigate the rest of my life never enjoying a daddy-daughter moment again? It broke me.

By the time I reached high school, my trauma had grown as tall as I was. But each day, I painted a smile on my face. Literally. My favorite lipstick color was cherry jubilee by Avon, which was also my mother's favorite. We wore it proudly. I can still remember how it stained the joint before I lost consciousness. It was laced.

There are certain details from that night that I do not remember, but I will never forget the look on the face of the teary-eyed firefighter who helped save my life. After I was stabilized in the hospital, we talked, and he made me promise never to experiment with drugs again. I agreed and kept my promise, sobered by the knowledge that the last child he saw in my condition had passed away.

It would take nearly thirty years for me to put my childhood "mistake" into context. I realized it was not a mistake at all but an attempt to self-medicate. I remember the moment of this epiphany. It came around the time that I began volunteering with a prison ministry program in Staunton, Virginia, helping women struggling with addiction.

After building relationships with women who had been locked up in jail or prison for a sickness they could not control, I began to ask myself: What could have become of my life if I had gotten high instead of hitting the floor? Might I have become a victim of the War on Drugs? Might my future possibilities have been stripped away, along with my citizenship rights? Might I have become a slave of the state?

At the end of my conversation with the women at the jail in New Orleans, I fully understood my purpose for writing this book and the personal journey that led me here. What started as a history lesson transformed into a lesson in courageous storytelling, which I offer you in *Searching for Jane Crow*.

INTRODUCTION

BLACK WOMEN, MASS INCARCERATION, AND THE LEGACIES OF SLAVERY

"They shipped me off just like they captured and shipped off my ancestors," Susan Burton recalled, describing her experience entering California's prison system. Her journey began in 1982 in the dark hours of the morning with a wake-up call from the sheriff.

"Get up, Burton. You're being transported," he ordered.

Susan's journey took her from a county jail to a women's prison, where she would spend years fighting for her freedom, but not before enduring a strip search and dehumanizing commands: "Open your mouth. Lift up your tongue. Pull your ear back. Lift up your arms. Let me see the soles of your feet. Bend over and cough." Her body was examined as if she were an enslaved person being readied for the auction block, then branded with a state-issued uniform with "Property of the State of California" stamped across the back. Then came the chains. "I was put in chains around my ankles and around my wrists, and I was marched out into a line on a bus," she told me.

After being designated as state property and given a number to replace her name, Susan was compelled to labor. "They classified me for work," she recalled. The prison authorities assessed her based on perceived physical abilities, which resulted in long hours spent raising chickens, mowing grass, and working in the "Big House"—a term incarcerated individuals often use for prison.

Susan received very little pay for her time. "They paid me eight cents an hour to keep up the prison, which doubled as the plantation, historically, and if I didn't cooperate and work, I would be put in the hole or solitary confinement," she reflected. "But in slavery days, I would have gotten whipped or put into the hot box." For Susan, serving time mirrored the harsh realities of chattel slavery. "It's just a twenty-first century replication of the eighteenth century," she concluded.

Before meeting Susan Burton and learning about her role as the founder of A New Way of Life Reentry Project, a national organization advocating for the freedom of and justice for incarcerated and formerly incarcerated women, I had never heard a Black woman describe her imprisonment as a form of enslavement. Despite decades of researching the impact of slavery's legacies on Black women, I had not grasped how deeply this reality persists today, nor how long this has been the case. Since the earliest years of America's founding, systems of incarceration and slavery have worked together to keep Black women bound.

Since hearing Susan's remarkable story and acute analysis, I have been on a quest to uncover the relationship between mass incarceration and slavery. This journey has led me to archives and libraries all over the United States, from Mississippi to Washington, DC. It has also taken me inside the living rooms of safe houses for women returning from prison and into jail classrooms that serve as chapels, where women gather to pray, testify, and tell their stories.

Interviewing survivors and learning about their stories made me reflect on the lives of the enslaved, particularly the experiences of those who suffered from imprisonment. It is sobering to realize that between 1810 and 1865 alone, an estimated one million enslaved people experienced incarceration in America's jails and prisons. At least one-third of them were women.

While writing this book, I realized that since the beginning of the United States, mass incarceration has been a persistent reality for Black Americans, even while hidden in the shadow of slavery. In fact, what started as an effort to highlight the invisibility of Black women ultimately revealed deeper insights about mass incarceration and slavery. These revelations have led me to ask new questions: What role did slavery play in the establishment of mass incarceration? How have these systems evolved over time? How does slavery's legacy of mass incarceration continue to affect the lives of Black Americans today?

I contemplated these questions as I searched through historical documents for answers, discovering some buried in nineteenth-century slave jail ledgers and runaway dockets (lists of individuals jailed for escaping slavery), others in prison registers and receipts for hiring enslaved chain gang laborers, and still others in city and county jail rosters. I read slave narratives, fugitive slave ads, freedom suits (lawsuits filed by enslaved individuals seeking freedom), and other records from the chattel slavery era. I uncovered other answers in post-Emancipation slave auction advertisements, convict leasing contracts, prison plantation records, whipping reports, reward posters, peonage case files (records documenting the enslavement of Black individuals for unpaid criminal fines and debts), parole contracts, census records, and personal narratives.

The personal narratives of Black women currently affected by mass incarceration have been crucial in helping me understand this history. I rely on their ability to express the unspoken and undocumented struggles of their incarcerated ancestors, as they are the only ones capable of articulating what it means to be both a prisoner and a slave and to navigate life as a citizen in chains. Their testimonies shed light on the challenges Black women faced in the past while also giving voice to the experiences of those now incarcerated in a system often called the new Jim Crow.

Today, the term "Jim Crow" is used to describe our modern-day system of mass incarceration, regarded by many as a new form of racial caste. In her groundbreaking book *The New Jim Crow*, Michelle Alexander powerfully explains the correlation: "Once you're labeled a felon, the old forms of discrimination—employment discrimination, housing discrimination, denial of the right to vote, denial of educational opportunity, denial of food stamps and other public benefits, and exclusion from jury service—are suddenly legal. As a criminal, you have scarcely more rights, and arguably less respect, than a black man living in Alabama at the height of Jim Crow."[1]

Since its publication, *The New Jim Crow* has transformed the way we understand mass incarceration and its profound effects on Black men, especially regarding the loss of citizenship. However, there is more to learn about this system. In this book, I argue that one hundred years before Jim Crow, Black women were subjected to "Jane Crow."[2] I use this term to describe the historical oppression faced by Black women due to their race and second-class freedom status. I also use the term to highlight the carceral consequences of this inequality across generations. *Searching for Jane Crow* offers new lessons into how racial biases within the legal system contributed to mass incarceration long before Black people had a right of citizenship to deny.

Searching for Jane Crow draws on methods common in the writing of Black women's history, using both established and new practices, including one recently developed by historians Daina Ramey Berry and Kali Nicole Gross. In *A Black Women's History of the United States*, these authors diverge from a traditional timeline of American history, opting instead for a chronology that is "most significant to Black women's lived experiences."[3]

I find this method relevant to my own writing as it allows me to focus on a timeline of American history centered on Black women and not the common narrative. To tell *this* story of the United States, I highlight key events that have shaped the history of Black women and mass incarceration, including the enforcement of the Fugitive Slave Acts, the rise of the domestic slave trade, the explosive growth of cotton, the ratification of the Thirteenth Amendment to the US Constitution, the resurgence of racial violence, the enforcement of legal segregation, the eradication of Black citizenship, the fight for equal freedom, and the War on Drugs.

This book offers a new perspective on mass incarceration, including its origins and its ongoing effects. It also reveals the importance of recounting this history from a Black woman's perspective. Their experiences offer a different viewpoint, enabling us to trace the roots of this system well before the 1970s. Listening closely to Black women has made me realize that mass incarceration began not with the War on Drugs but with slavery.

Before the dramatic rise of the US prison population during the late twentieth century, Black women had already experienced mass incarceration. Hundreds of thousands were held in slave jails as part of the domestic slave trade, a system that trafficked enslaved individuals throughout the Southern United States. Thousands more were detained in city jails for escaping from enslavement or for failing to prove they were legally free.[4]

Even after the ratification of the Thirteenth Amendment in 1865, Black women continued to endure mass incarceration. Instead of being imprisoned under a system of chattel slavery, they were enslaved within the carceral system. Although the Thirteenth Amendment abolished slavery in the United States, it allowed for its continuation "as a punishment for crime." This had a profound impact on Black women, no longer considered private property but subjected to becoming state property.

While researching this book, I immediately noticed the deep historical influence of slavery's legacies on mass incarceration. However, it took me years to realize how this system began. As it turns out, slavery caused mass incarceration. And from its earliest days, mass incarceration has been used to perpetuate slavery. This insight has completely transformed my perspective on these systems. No longer do I view them as isolated institutions; I now see them as interconnected systems of racial control. I have also changed my understanding of the timeline of mass incarceration. Instead of viewing it as a recent historical development, I now recognize it as a practice that has existed for over two hundred years.

Evidence of mass incarceration's enduring existence can be found in some of America's most fundamental documents: the US Constitution, the Fugitive Slave Acts of 1793 and 1850, and the Violent Crime Control and Law Enforcement Act of 1994, also known as the Clinton Crime Bill. It is also evident in the histories of Black women who endured the oppression caused by these laws and policies. Their challenges and efforts to overcome America's system of criminal injustice form the heart of this book.

Searching for Jane Crow tells the story of how Black women became the most punished group of women in the United States. It is the first comprehensive history of Black women and mass incarceration, spanning three centuries, from the domestic slave trade in the early 1800s to our current system of mass imprisonment. Unlike other books that focus on Black men, this book traces the history through Black women's experiences.

There are still very few books on the history of Black women's incarceration. Two of the most notable are Kali Nicole Gross's *Colored Amazons: Crime, Violence, and Black Women in the City of Brotherly Love, 1880–1910* and Cheryl D. Hicks's *Talk with You Like a Woman: African American Women, Justice, and Reform in New York, 1890–1935*. These books provide insight into the imprisonment of Black women in the North, reshaping our understanding of the history of America's prisons and their role in the founding of the nation. My book contributes further to this story.

Searching for Jane Crow reveals that while the North may have been home to the nation's earliest prison systems, the South was the birthplace of mass incarceration. This region imprisoned more Black people than in any other part of the United States—and more Black women than any other group of women.

While most books about the history of mass incarceration start with the War on Drugs, this narrative begins with the expansion of slavery. During the late seventeenth and eighteenth centuries, chattel slavery existed in most American colonies, but it was most prevalent in a region known as the Upper South. In this area, enslavers exploited Black people's labor to produce tobacco, a crop that once served as the foundation of the agricultural economy and a key source of America's wealth. By the early 1800s, however, the tobacco industry declined steeply, and cotton became the nation's leading commodity.

The cotton gin, introduced in 1793, transformed the cotton industry by accelerating production: A task that once required enslaved people to remove seeds from fiber by hand could now be done by machine. As a result, America's reliance on slavery increased, particularly in Alabama, Georgia, Mississippi, Louisiana, Arkansas, and Texas—a region called the Deep South.

The rise of the cotton industry occurred at a crucial time. The tobacco fields of the Upper South had dried up, leaving enslavers with a surplus of enslaved people and an opportunity to set them free. However, most chose not to. Instead, they sold their enslaved laborers to the Deep South—a decision that changed the course of American history, bringing about a new system of slave trading and the country's first system of mass incarceration.

In 1808, the US government banned the Atlantic slave trade to America. While this meant it was no longer legal to import human beings from overseas, enslavers could buy and sell them through the domestic slave trade.

The domestic slave trade, often called the internal slave trade or the Second Middle Passage, involved the commercial transport of enslaved individuals from the Upper South, primarily Virginia, Washington, DC, and Maryland, to states in the Deep South. Unlike the Atlantic slave trade, this system of slave trading occurred exclusively on US soil. Its devastation, however, was no less severe. Whether taken from the nation's capital or the coast of West Africa, enslaved people endured the trauma of being separated from their loved ones and stripped of the only lives they knew.

The internal slave trade was essential in expanding chattel slavery and played a significant role in escalating incarceration. To facilitate the transport of nearly one million enslaved individuals, slave traders built a new system of private slave jails. They put these jails in cities where the slave trade flourished, including Richmond, Virginia; Alexandria, Virginia; Baltimore, Maryland; Washington, DC; Memphis, Tennessee; Montgomery, Alabama; New Orleans, Louisiana; and Natchez, Mississippi. In the process, they established a multimillion-dollar punishment industry we now recognize as mass incarceration.

Cotton, not crack, was the primary driver of mass incarceration in its earliest years. And slave jails, not prisons, were its first for-profit institutions. More than mere warehouses for storing human property, slave jails served as a crucial link between slavery and incarceration, uniting two oppressive systems of captivity with a common objective: profit.

The jailing of enslaved people for profit is central to the origins of mass incarceration. A desire to commodify Black people's bodies, not crime, spurred this epidemic. Before 1865, most imprisoned Black individuals in America had never been arrested or convicted of any offense. Being trafficked through the domestic slave trade, not criminal behavior, led to their imprisonment.

During the domestic slave trading era, incarceration became closely associated with race. The mass imprisonment of enslaved individuals strengthened this connection, as did the racialized enforcement of slavery; as the institution of slavery grew stronger so did the laws governing race and punishment. Although racially charged legislation existed before the domestic slave trade, these laws were more widely enforced after its establishment.

Slave codes and "Black Laws" (discriminatory laws targeting free Black people) imposed race-based penalties, including imprisonment for enslaved individuals who escaped to freedom and free persons who exercised their legal right to it. Through these laws, Southern state governments initiated what I would call a War on Black Freedom. To fight this war, they received support from the federal government, marking the first time the United States directly participated in the spread of mass incarceration through the enactment of federal anti-freedom laws known as the Fugitive Slave Acts.

The Fugitive Slave Acts, passed by Congress in 1793 and 1850, permitted the capture and return of enslaved people who fled from one state to another. This legislation significantly contributed to the protection of slavery through incarceration. One could argue that the institution of slavery might not have survived without a system of mass jailing to safeguard it. For the first time in American history, the Fugitive Slave Acts codified race-based incarceration at the federal level, providing law enforcement, state representatives, and citizens the power to arrest, charge, and commit enslaved people to jail if they escaped.[5]

Jails played a vital role in punishing the enslaved. And they protected the economic interests of enslavers. Functioning as a tool for both punishment and profit, they helped to recover millions of dollars' worth of lost human beings. Yet for the enslaved, it meant enduring the dehumanizing experience of being treated as commodities and "criminals" under the law.

Prior to the Fugitive Slave Acts, many Southern states already had runaway laws, which targeted enslaved people and heightened their surveillance. The acts advanced this trend by monitoring the movement of escaped individuals to northern cities, where many free Black individuals lived and where large numbers of self-liberated people made their way to freedom. The once well-traveled paths to safety became routes to confinement. Although there are no records documenting the exact number of enslaved individuals incarcerated for attempting to escape slavery, it is conservatively estimated that at least ten thousand people were jailed for this nonviolent "crime." This number includes those who might now be called repeat "offenders"—individuals for whom the jail's bars didn't curb their determination to be free.

History shows the devastating impact that mass incarceration had on the lives of enslaved people. It also deeply affected the experiences of free Black individuals. Unfortunately, the laws that granted their legal right to liberty did not effectively protect it. As long as slavery existed, genuine freedom could not be realized for the countless free Black women and men falsely accused of being runaway slaves.

Like their enslaved counterparts, free Black women faced threats of imprisonment and oppressive laws that criminalized every aspect of their lives. Owning a weapon, breaking curfew, traveling without free papers, and socializing with an enslaved person without the permission of their owner or overseer could send a free Black woman to jail. A Black woman's implied connection to enslavement, or what I call a "chattel history," led to restrictions on her freedom, much like a criminal record does today.[6]

Even though free Black women had free legal status, they did not possess full rights to freedom. At best, they experienced a form of second-class freedom, a limited freedom reserved for Black people. Unlike the complete freedom enjoyed by white Americans, this form of liberty did not come with permanent guarantees. It was probationary, requiring monetary payments to access and maintain.

For a Black woman to become free, she usually had to purchase herself out of bondage and obtain a freedom certificate.[7] Following that, she had to continually renew her freedom with the county court, like a vehicle registration. She could expect serious legal penalties if she failed, ranging from several months of imprisonment to the permanent loss of liberty. *Even before the framers of the Thirteenth Amendment gathered to discuss the future of Black freedom, Black women were already being enslaved as a punishment for crime.*

The criminal legal system played a crucial role in enforcing second-class freedom, a status that not only undermined Black women's liberty but also restricted their access to citizenship. Before the ratification of the Fourteenth Amendment to the US Constitution in 1868, Black individuals lacked citizenship rights and the essential condition for it: complete freedom. This lack of equal freedom was central to the Supreme Court's 1857 Dred Scott decision, which ruled that enslaved people—and free Black people—were not citizens and therefore had none of the rights or privileges of citizenship. But decades prior, the practice of denying citizenship rights to Black individuals already existed. As historian Martha Jones explains, although the 1787 Constitution did not formally legislate Black anti-citizenship at the federal level, "most authorities leaned toward the view that color, with its implied link to slave status, disqualified Black Americans from citizenship."[8]

After Black Americans gained the right to citizenship through the Fourteenth Amendment, white Southerners aimed to suppress it, upholding the view that Black people's blackness made them ineligible for it. After a twenty-eight-year battle to eradicate Black citizenship, white Southerners prevailed. The *Plessy v. Ferguson* Supreme Court ruling in 1896 ultimately denied equal rights for Black Americans, determining that state-mandated segregation laws did not violate the equal protection clause of the Fourteenth Amendment. This decision solidified racial discrimination in America, resulting in a system often called Jim Crow.

As noted, I use "Jane Crow" to refer to the historical oppression faced by Black women due to their race and second-class freedom status a century before Jim Crow. Enslaved women experienced these consequences in the form of imprisonment for seeking freedom, while free women were incarcerated under restrictive laws on their liberty. Even after federal laws supported equal freedom after 1865, Black women continued to face incarceration for exercising it. A "crime" as trivial as quitting a white employer could result in jail time. Today, thousands of incarcerated and formerly incarcerated Black women still struggle for access to this basic human right. For them, Jane Crow's inequalities have meant confronting oppressive barriers created by felony convictions. It has also meant having their fundamental right to freedom treated as a racial privilege.

With these realities in mind, I write this book. My aim is not to show how mass incarceration functions as a racial caste system that affects Black women. Rather, it is to examine how the historical denial of Black women's right to freedom led to mass incarceration long before the term was ever coined.

Searching for Jane Crow provides a new history of mass incarceration. It contributes to an ongoing effort to understand how this system emerged, acknowledging that no single interpretation can fully explain it. However, this book does not claim to represent the experiences of all groups of Americans. Its main purpose is to shine a light on Black women, who have been historically overlooked, and to share their untold stories.

This book begins with the stories of Black women who were mass incarcerated during the period of chattel slavery. Chapter 1, "Finding Jane Crow," explores their journey through the early years of America's founding, from the domestic slave trade to the end of the Civil War. It follows Black women behind the walls of the nation's first private slave jails and into its public jails and state prisons. Moreover, it examines how the expansion of slavery and the increase in race-based imprisonment impacted Black women, revealing the often overlooked origins of mass incarceration.

Chapter 2, "Freedom's Aftermath," follows Black women from the end of chattel slavery to the beginning of legal freedom. During this period in American history, approximately four million people were released from slavery and imprisonment in slave jails. It was an era marked by hope, optimism, and opportunity as Black women experienced having their liberty protected by federal law for the first time. But for the white Southerners invested in holding them in chains, it represented a loss that could only be restored through lethal violence and racially biased laws, such as the Black Codes. The ratification of equal freedom and citizenship did not bring racial equality; instead, it laid the foundation for an ongoing war against Black freedom.

Black women emerged from slavery as legally free individuals but without the full protections of citizenship. They were granted the promise of lifetime liberty but remained at risk of being re-enslaved. Chapter 3, "Debt Slavery," explores the transition to enslavement through the carceral system. It documents the emergence of a second era of mass incarceration for Black women following the Civil War, chronicling how mass jailing was used to perpetuate their enslavement. Exploiting Black women's free labor on chain gangs, on plantations, and in private households while charging them for their freedom through hard work or cash payments became a standard practice in post–Thirteenth Amendment America. Punishment for profit became a defining feature of America's criminal legal system during this period, most evident within the prison system.

For a Black woman convicted of a felony after 1865, imprisonment meant enslavement to the state prison system followed by being leased out to private contractors through the convict leasing system. It also meant being put to work on a state-run prison farm or plantation. Today, it means being confined within the walls of a private or state prison as property, working for minimal compensation—if any—while profits increase and the costs of one's incarceration accumulate. Chapter 4, "Profiting Prisons," explores how state-sponsored mass incarceration has perpetuated slavery from the end of the Civil War to the War on Drugs. It details how Black individuals transitioned from being considered chattel to becoming citizens and then, ultimately, state property. This chapter also examines the expansion of America's punishment industry since its peak during the domestic slave trade, showing how slavery's legacy of mass incarceration continues to shape our carceral system today.

The auction block, once the primary site of family separation and sale, has been replaced by the Adoption and Safe Families Act. Public jails and prisons have emerged as key facilitators of family separation in mass incarceration's current era. Chapter 5, "Family Separation," examines the human cost of this system, showing how it perpetuates slavery through the separation of families for profit. By investigating the historical roots of this issue, this chapter provides new insights into how slavery influences the child "welfare" system, exposing its hidden impact on incarcerated mothers and the children they are forced to leave behind.

Mass incarceration continues the legacy of slavery in other significant ways, including through the system of parole. Historically, this system upheld the conditions of enslavement and imposed requirements such as forced labor, fines, fees, and other forms of compensation necessary to maintain one's second-class freedom. Chapter 6, "Tracking Freedom," examines the history of Black women's experiences with parole, or "supervised freedom." It details their struggle to pay the high costs of freedom and overcome the enslavement they've endured in pursuit of it.

Searching for Jane Crow concludes by suggesting solutions for achieving freedom that shift the focus from punishment to liberty. It emphasizes the belief that reform is an ineffective way to address mass incarceration. Just as chattel slavery could not be improved, mass incarceration cannot be fixed. Until this system is abolished, slavery will persist.

SEARCHING FOR JANE CROW

CHAPTER 1

FINDING JANE CROW

"Dem days was hell," Delia Garlic recalled. "Babies was snatched from dere mother's breas' an' sold to speculators [slave traders]. Chilluns was separated from sisters an' brothers an' never saw each other ag'in . . . It's bad to belong to folks dat own you soul an' body; dat can tie you up to a tree, wid yo' arms fastened tight aroun' it; who take a long curlin' whip an' cut de blood ever' lick."[1]

Delia was born into slavery in Powhatan, Virginia, in the 1830s at the height of the domestic slave trade. She was the youngest of thirteen children, the last to be sold away from her mother. As a little girl, she witnessed the auction of at least one of her siblings, her older brother William: "Him an' my mother an' me was brought in a speculator's drove to Richmon' [Virginia] an' put in a warehouse [slave jail] wid a drove of other n——s. Den we was all put on a block an' sol' to de highes' bidder. I never seed brother William ag'in."

One can only imagine the pain and fear that Delia felt, watching her brother sold and taken away. The helplessness she must have suffered watching her mother weep over William. The disgust she experienced when the trader greased her lips to give buyers the impression that she was well-fed. And the humiliation she endured as strange men stuck their dirty fingers into her mouth to check the soundness of her teeth.

The county sheriff purchased Delia and her mother at the Richmond auction to work in his home, where Delia suffered physical abuse at the hands of his daughter and wife. On one occasion, the sheriff's daughter picked up a hot iron and ran it down her arm. "It took off de flesh when she done it," Delia recalled. On a separate occasion, her mistress picked up a piece of firewood and threw it at her, knocking her unconscious.[2]

Delia "kept on stayin' dere," at the sheriff's place, until she couldn't take it anymore. She ran away after he threatened to sic the overseer on her. "I began to cry an' run an' run in de night: but finally I run back to de quarters an' heard mammy callin' me," she remembered. "I has thought many times through all dese years how mammy looked dat night. She pressed my han' in bofe of hers an' said 'Be good an' trus' in de Lawd.'" That night, Delia was taken to Richmond and sold to another slave trader. She never saw her mother again.

Delia experienced incarceration in the slave jail and was put on the auction block a second time. A hotel owner in McDonough, Georgia, purchased her on credit. According to Delia, "[W]hen de time come aroun' to pay for me, his hotel done fail. Den de Atlanta man dat bought de hotel bought me too. 'Fo' long, dough, I was sol' to a man by de name of Garlic, down in Louisiana, an' I stayed wid him 'till I was freed."[3]

Delia was sold three times and made two trips to the private slave jails of Richmond. Each time, she slept behind a wall around sixteen feet tall, in a crowded cell filled with women, men, and children dreading being sold to the Deep South. A brick floor was her bed. A heavy weight of worry was her cover. She was kept up at night by the sound of hearts breaking and shed tears pounding the floor.

Delia's story shows how enslaved people navigated between the plantation and the private jail, between slavery and incarceration. They suffered what historian Daina Ramey Berry calls a "double incarceration," the experience of being caught between two systems of captivity. This dual oppression was unique to the enslaved in the same way that chattel slavery—a system that allowed for Africans to be bought, sold, and enslaved forever—differed from other forms of slavery in the global world such as serfdom in Europe and debt bondage in Asia.

In this book, I argue that mass incarceration has its roots in slavery and is fundamentally built on a historical foundation of racism. Understanding the story of slavery in America is impossible without also addressing the story of mass incarceration. The domestic slave trade serves as the crucial beginning of this narrative, tracing the nation's early involvement in racially motivated, profit-driven imprisonment.

Originating in the early nineteenth century, slave jails played a key role in introducing profit-based incarceration into the existing antebellum carceral system. Unlike other carceral institutions in America, these jails were designed solely to generate wealth for slave traders who also served as jailers. To clarify, slave traders owned both the jails and the people confined within them. Trading firms invested in constructing these facilities to temporarily detain enslaved individuals purchased from local enslavers for resale in the Deep South. They also supported independent traders who lacked their own jails by contracting with them, for a fee, to store their human "stock."

Functioning as more than mere warehouses, slave jails were an essential part of America's early carceral system. They were its first commercial carceral institutions, existing long before the boom of the private prison industry in the 1980s and 1990s, and the founding of private prison companies. Based on this fact, one could argue that the corporatization of incarceration has its roots in private slave jails and in the domestic slave trade, not in private prisons.

Considering the importance of enslaved people's experiences to the history of mass incarceration, one is left to wonder why they have been ignored. Is it because they don't count as "real" prisoners and slave jails don't count as carceral spaces? Is it because we don't believe that a person could be both enslaved *and* incarcerated at the same time? Or is it possible that we have accepted the notion that enslaved people were simply commodities, and that being owned by an enslaver somehow shielded them from becoming victims of the antebellum criminal legal system?[4]

Before the Civil War, hundreds of thousands of enslaved women experienced imprisonment in America's jails and prisons. However, countless free Black women also endured the carceral consequences of slavery. Women such as Lauisa Brown, a "free Mulattoe," who was taken from the city jail in Richmond, Virginia, to the "old [slave] market" and placed on the auction block.[5]

Police arrested Lauisa for failing to register as a free person in the Commonwealth of Virginia, where she spent six months in jail fighting for her freedom. During this time, she accumulated $67.15 worth of jail fees, the equivalent of approximately $2,406.67 today.[6] She learned that freedom came with a hidden cost that she could not afford to pay. On an order from the Hustings Court, she was hired out to John J. Mountcastel "for so long a time as may be necessary to pay jail fees." A period of *fifty years*.[7]

The story of Black women's mass incarceration begins in the early nineteenth-century South. Its origins can be traced to city jails, slave jails, and prisons where hundreds of thousands of Black women were locked away for petty "crimes," or for simply having Black skin; most Black prisoners, when you consider those confined in Southern slave jails, were never convicted of any crime.

Delia Garlic and Lauisa Brown represent the many enslaved and free Black women who were incarcerated not due to any wrongdoing, but because of the factors related to the expansion of slavery and the racialized incarceration it caused. Their stories, and the stories of so many others, are central to our understanding of the history of Black women and mass incarceration. They help us understand the origins of this epidemic and its enduring impact on Black women today.

Chapter 1, "Finding Jane Crow," documents Black women's journey through mass incarceration's first era, from the beginning of the domestic slave trade to the end of the Civil War. It follows these women through slave auctions, cell blocks, and chain gangs, showing the wide range of their experiences—from being confined in a slave jail for weeks to being sold by a public jail for a lifetime. From receiving a life sentence in prison to giving life to a child who would be sold into slavery, the story of Black women and mass incarceration begins.

In 1834, during the Christmas holidays, Malinda, "a mulatto slave girl," married the love of her life, Henry. To be in a "union of feeling" and not a forced coupling was a privilege they both cherished. Malinda and Henry chose each other, knowing their bond could be broken at any time. They understood that their sacred pledge was a "temporary matter" and slave marriages were "without license or sanction or law."[8]

When Henry asked about their future together, Malinda told him, "I have always felt a desire to be free; I have long cherished a hope that I should yet be free, either by purchase or running away." She expressed how her longing for freedom made her reluctant to "enter the married state while a slave." The couple married anyway, on the condition that they would "embrace the earliest opportunity of running away to Canada."[9]

Malinda shared her freedom dreams with Henry, but life under "Master" Gatewood was nothing but nightmares. Until they lived together on Gatewood's plantation in Oldham County, Kentucky, Henry did not know the extent of his sweetheart's suffering. He had never seen her "exposed to the insults and licentious passions of wicked slave-drivers and overseers." He had never watched her bear the stripes of the lash.

After their first anniversary, Malinda and Henry welcomed a baby girl whom they named Mary Frances. Her adoring father described her as "a pretty child; she was quiet, playful, bright, and interesting." She had sparkling eyes like her mother, but at times, they were hard to see behind the bruises surrounding them.

While Malinda worked in the fields, "there was no one [to] take care of poor little Frances." She was "left at the house to creep under the feet of an unmerciful old mistress." One summer afternoon, "Frances came creeping to her mother smiling, but with large tear drops standing in her dear little eyes . . . Her little face was bruised Black with the whole print of Mrs. Gatewood's hand." When Henry looked upon his daughter who had been "whipped and tortured with impunity," and his wife who endured acts of cruelty that he could not find "decent language" to describe, he felt powerless and broken. On Christmas Day 1837, Henry ran away.[10]

Henry returned to rescue his family, then left again without them. He was captured in Cincinnati and taken to a "justice office," but according to Henry, "it was more like an office of injustice." The proslavery judge had him returned to the plantation.

Henry made one last attempt to rescue Malinda and Mary Frances, which resulted in the entire family being jailed and sold. Madison Garrison, a slave trader, bought Henry and his family and took them to a workhouse in Louisville, Kentucky, to be "kept under lock and key at work" until Garrison acquired enough human property to "take off to the South."[11]

Malinda and Mary Frances were put inside a "very large brick building . . . built on the plan of a jail or state's prison, with many apartments to it, divided into cells." It was "enclosed by a high stone wall" surrounded by "watchmen with loaded guns to guard the prisoners from breaking out, and on either side there were large iron gates."[12]

Henry thought of "hell, with all of its terrors of torment" when he entered this place of punishment (Malinda must have thought the same). He was astonished to see so many "whites as well as colored men loaded down with irons, at hard labor, under the supervision of overseers." He was even more perplexed by the presence of enslaved people who, according to Henry, were "there without crime."[13]

After Malinda and Henry did time in the Louisville workhouse, they were carried to the New Orleans slave market, where they endured another incarceration, this time in a slave jail. After working on multiple plantations in Louisiana, their union was broken, just as they feared it would be. The couple never made it to Canada, and they never experienced freedom together. Their love story ends with Malinda being sold as a sex slave in the nineteenth-century domestic slave trade.

Following the abolition of the transatlantic slave trade to the United States in 1808, the domestic slave trade emerged. It affected an estimated one million Black people, who were forcibly migrated from the Upper South states of Maryland, Virginia, Delaware, Kentucky, Tennessee, and North Carolina, and the District of Columbia, and sold in states and territories in the Deep South.[14] With the cotton boom came an increased demand for enslaved laborers—and jails to confine them.

Itinerant slave traders, also called "soul traders" and "soul drivers," combed the countryside looking for people to buy. They met with enslavers and attended local courthouse sales, where they purchased small batches of human "chattel" to sell in the city for a higher price. Other traders formed lucrative trading firms and made a fortune off the trade in human souls.

Slave-collecting and resale centers existed in several urban cities in the Upper South, including Richmond, Virginia; Baltimore, Maryland; and Alexandria, Virginia.[15] Yet the nation's largest and wealthiest slave-trading firm belonged to Isaac Franklin and John Armfield who, from 1828 to 1836, dominated the "human flesh market." They sold more people (over one thousand a year), broke up more families, and made more money from the domestic trade than any other soul trader in America. They traded on cash and credit, their yearly revenue exceeding $200,000. The pair amassed assets worth billions in today's dollars.

The headquarters of the Franklin and Armfield slave-trading firm in Alexandria, Virginia, doubled as home to one of the most infamous slave jails in America. The number of people who passed through its grated iron doors far exceeded that of any ordinary slave jail. While an average facility might have held 30 to 40 individuals at a time, this one could accommodate over 140.[16]

Ethan Allen Andrews, a prominent American educator, marveled at the jail's tall whitewashed buildings, barred windows, padlocked gates, and heavy stone walls during a visit in 1836. Although the "slave pen" bore all the features of a prison, he found it to be worse: "In most respects . . . the situation of the convicts at the penitentiary was far less deplorable than that of these slaves, confined for the crime of being descended from ancestors who were forcibly reduced to bondage. Most of the former are confined for a few years only, and then go forth as free. . . . Far different is the condition of the slave. He is a prisoner for life."[17]

Andrews encountered "thirty or forty female slaves" on his visit to the slave trader's supermax. But he never encountered Franklin and Armfield's "fancy maids," women who were sold as sex commodities or held for a lifetime as sex slaves. As historian Edward Baptist powerfully explains, "Franklin and his colleagues passionately wanted 'mulatto' women, and Black people generally: as bodies to rape and bodies to sell."[18]

After being detained for weeks at a time, slaves began the journey down south. Women, men, and children of all ages traveled hundreds of miles to their destinations, on foot and in chains. They marched bound together in a coffle, which abolitionist Harriet Tubman described as a "chain gang."[19] Meanwhile, the "drivers" who led these forced migrations rode in wagons with shotguns and single-horse carriages.

Franklin and Armfield transported their victims overland and on tightly packed steamboats and ships. In 1829, the firm owned at least one vessel. By 1835, they commanded a fleet: the *United States*, the *Tribune*, the *Uncas*, and the *Isaac Franklin*.[20] One can only imagine what this journey along the Atlantic Coast was like for those forced to endure it. How did they handle the rough currents, strong winds, and rain? How did they survive the beatings, the hunger, and the sickness?

For many, the tumultuous journey ended in New Orleans, the largest slave-trading center in the Deep South and home to the highest number of traders. According to historian Maurie McInnis, "In the 1856 directory, there were 17 individuals or businesses listed as slave trader and another 38 listed as auctioneers, many of whom probably sold slaves."[21] Today's Omni Royal Orleans Hotel stands on the site where thousands of enslaved people were once auctioned.

The "slave prison" on the corner of Saint Joseph Street in the famous French Quarter was a "resort" for traders and enslavers who came from cities, towns, and parishes near and far to purchase human souls. Every day at ten o'clock, enslaved people had to prepare themselves for the auction block. They started by combing their hair and washing their faces. If someone appeared too "dark and rough," they were forced to take the extra step of washing in greasy dishwater, as if scrubbing with oil and lye could erase the pain and degradation of being sold.[22] Meanwhile, mothers carefully dressed their young, almost as if preparing them for burial, knowing they might never see them again.

By midday, every man, woman, and child was taken from the "slave pen" to the "trader's yard." They were forced to line up, "stand up straight," and "look as sprightly as they could," even as the buyers groped their bodies and subjected them to sexualized abuse. One witness recalled, "[The men would] walk up and down 'tween the two rows and grab a woman and try to throw her down and feel of her to see how she's put up. If she's purty strong, he'd say, 'Is she a good breeder?'"[23]

Buyers paid an average of $515 for women of childbearing age.[24] Wombs were valuable; the plantation economy could not grow without them. Enslaved women were appraised based on their ability to produce children *and* crops. To convince speculators to buy them, the enslaved women had to answer questions about their worth or suffer a beating if they refused. They had to dance, jump, and sing when they wanted to run, hide, and scream.

"Oh Lord Jesus, how long, how long shall I suffer this way!" shouted one woman as she watched her son being sold to an enslaver. She fell at the feet of the man who had just purchased her, "clung to his knees," and begged him to buy her baby "and spare her one, at least, of her little ones." He responded with "violent blows and kicks as to reduce her to the necessity of creeping out of his reach and mingling the groan of bodily suffering with the sob of a breaking heart."[25]

When Eliza's water broke, her dream came crashing down, heavy as the leg irons restraining her every move and reminding her of her enslavement. In 1849, the day after she was imprisoned for attempting to escape, she gave birth to a baby girl. The District of Columbia (or DC) Jail was not the place she imagined bringing her daughter into the world. She hoped to deliver her in freedom.[26]

Eliza and her newborn were jailed for four weeks, while others remained in the DC Jail days, months, or years. Between 1848 and 1854, at least three hundred Black women—both free and enslaved—served time in the DC Jail. But hundreds more were "living" there. A keeper of the jail stated that "in five years [between 1831 and 1836] upwards of *four hundred and fifty* colored persons had been lodged there for *safekeeping*, i.e. until they could be disposed of in the course of the slave trade;—besides nearly *three hundred*, who had been taken up and lodged there as runaways."[27] Many of those detained claimed to be free.

Runaway dockets and jail registers are filled with the names of Black women and men who were incarcerated for seeking their freedom. I have personally traced thousands of individuals through these records, and every one of them who was jailed was charged with a nonviolent "crime." These so-called crimes were rooted in the desire for freedom—freedom of movement, freedom from abuse, freedom from family separation, freedom from surveillance, and freedom from slavery itself. They were put in chains to protect the investment enslavers had in their bodies. This also included those confined by their enslavers under a practice known as "safekeeping," in which enslavers paid the jail to hold their enslaved laborers, and to detain "runaways" until the enslavers could reclaim them.

In the summer of 1833, Fanny Jackson was captured and imprisoned in the DC Jail. She spent nearly two years confined in a cell with her three small children, Louisa, Robert, and Maria. The youngest child was still "an infant at her breast." Her husband was imprisoned too, held in a separate cell while the family awaited trial.

A legal violation led to Fanny's incarceration, but she had not committed a crime. Her enslavers, Ariss and Bernard Buckner, broke the law by taking the Jackson family across the Virginia line into the District of Columbia. They kept them there in violation of the 1796 Maryland law prohibiting the importation of slaves.[28] Maryland's nonimportation law, giving enslavers exactly one year to establish "bona fide" residency, applied in DC. During this period, they were expected to move their furniture, family heirlooms, prize possessions, and human property into the district. Fanny knew the law and intended to sue for her freedom. When the Buckners discovered her plan, they jailed the entire family and falsely claimed they had tried to escape.

From the confines of her cell, Fanny sued her enslaver on the grounds of having been illegally removed from the Commonwealth of Virginia into the District of Columbia, where she lived for several years unclaimed by her enslavers.[29] She felt she had a right to be free—and she did. And so did her husband and children. But the judge was of a different opinion. He ruled in favor of the Buckners.

Rachel Turner was just one year away from receiving her freedom when Mrs. Bromley decided to sell her to another enslaver. She would be forced to spend a lifetime in bondage to Angt. de Nanteuil. Or would she? Nanteuil took Rachel to the DC Jail under the pretense of "safekeeping," and she never saw him again. Months later, she was "sold for her jail fees, as a slave for life."[30]

The system of chattel slavery and the carceral system in the antebellum South were mutually dependent. Enslavers relied on jailers to protect their assets in their absence. And jailers relied on enslavers to pay jail fees to offset the cost of punishing their human property.

Like private jails, public jails profited from incarcerating so-called fugitive slaves and free Black people for a fee and from selling them into slavery. Based on my analysis of 139 enslaved women admitted to the DC Jail between May 1848 and December 1850, enslavers paid around $720.94 in jail fees. The average amount charged, per person, was five dollars, or $210 in today's currency. There is no way to determine how much buyers paid to purchase those sold for unpaid debt.[31]

In the city of Baltimore, the practice of charging fees to "protect" enslavers' human property was equally common, and so was imprisonment. Baltimore factors significantly in the early history of mass incarceration, as it possessed the largest free Black population of any city in America during the nineteenth century; in 1850 alone, 25,442 free Black people resided there, 14,610 of which were free Black women.[32] For individuals escaping enslavement, Baltimore offered a safe place to hide, though the threat of incarceration loomed constantly.

Between 1836 and 1864, a total of 2,228 Black individuals were arrested and incarcerated in the Baltimore City Jail for allegedly attempting to escape enslavement. Among them, 537 were women.[33] During the nineteenth century, the desire for freedom became the leading reason for "crime" in the city and the state, resulting in disproportionately high rates of incarceration for both enslaved and free Black people. This trend was also evident elsewhere, particularly in New Orleans, which was a major hub of the domestic slave trade and a leader in the punishment industry.

In New Orleans, home to the largest slave market in America, enslavers profited by renting their enslaved laborers to the city's police jail (a facility run by the police agency and the jail administration), which, in turn, exploited them on chain gangs. Between 1827 and 1835, 138 slaveholders in Louisiana—40 of whom were women—leased their enslaved workers. By contracting with the jail rather than private individuals, they expanded their slaveholding operations and accumulated wealth at the city's expense.

Those who had a surplus of enslaved labor leased out their excess workers to the city when they did not need them in the sugarcane fields. This allowed them to continue earning money without incurring the costs of maintaining their entire enslaved workforce. For widows, who frequently appear on chain gang registers, leasing enslaved laborers provided additional advantages. They could use the income to pay off debts left after their husband's deaths instead of selling their human assets.

Historical records show a significant presence of enslaved women on the chain gang. At least 703 women are listed on chain gang registers, though their specific labor roles are not detailed. From my extensive research on the history of Black women and chain gangs after 1865, it is safe to assume that enslaved women likewise contributed to the building and improvement of New Orleans' infrastructure and appearance. They would have helped repair streets and levees, sweep sidewalks, and clear trash from the street. And most importantly, they would have earned profits for their enslavers.

In 1833, Sandy spent 106 days on the chain gang, earning her enslaver, Lavergne, $26.50, which would be approximately $1,000 today. That same year, Matilde's thirty-four-day incarceration earned her enslaver $8.50.[34] While private individuals profited most from leasing their enslaved laborers to the chain gang, companies also cashed in on this practice.

Like private individuals, companies also owned enslaved people. The New Orleans-based architectural firm of Claude Gurlie and Joseph Guillot provides one example. These French-born architects are best known for constructing the College of Orleans, the first institution of higher learning in Louisiana, in 1811, as well as other New Orleans landmarks and private residences. However, in addition to their architectural work, they exploited enslaved laborers, hiring them out to the city jail.

Sophie spent 1,012 days confined to the chain gang. The city paid Gurlie and Guillot $253 to hire her; that's equivalent to $9,750 today.[35] She was not the only woman the firm leased for profit. They also rented enslaved laborers Betsie and Julie.

Although much has been written about the hiring of enslaved people to plantations, private residences, and businesses, the practice of leasing enslaved individuals to carceral institutions is scarcely mentioned in historical literature. With the rise of the domestic slave trade and for-profit jailing, one is left to wonder how deeply the punishment industry relied on slave hiring. Given the prevalence of slave chain gangs in New Orleans, it is evident that enslavers profited from the carceral system in ways that historians may never fully understand.

The domestic slave trade led to the establishment of private jails and an increased reliance on public jails for capturing "runaways." Slave traders used buildings, warehouses, federal-style homes, and other structures to imprison enslaved individuals before selling them to the Deep South. While private jails primarily existed to traffic enslaved people, they also acted as holding facilities for those who had attempted escape. Similar to public jails—where most "fugitive slaves" were sent—these institutions reinforced chattel slavery in areas where the system was vulnerable.

Slavery did not eliminate the need for jails. Instead, they expanded, and slavery helped justify their existence. The Fugitive Slave Acts, a pair of federal laws passed by Congress in 1793 and 1850 that authorized the capture and return of enslaved people who escaped from one state to another, would not have succeeded without jails. Without jails, there was no way to track enslaved people who "stole" their freedom or to enforce slavery itself. Incarceration became a tool to protect the "peculiar institution."

Enslavers posted advertisements in the classified sections of newspapers and in public places, offering cash rewards for the capture and confinement of those who had escaped from slavery. "Fugitive slave" ads read like wanted posters:

> $25 reward will be given for the apprehension and confinement in the jail of this county, of MARY and her daughter LOUISA, who ran off last Friday carrying their clothes with them
>
> FANNY RAN AWAY. Two days since . . . Five dollars will be paid for information to the conviction of any person who may employ or harbor her, and Three dollars for her delivery in the Work-House
>
> RANAWAY in May last, a Negro Girl named LAVENIA, about 18 years old, Black rough skin, thick lips, good teeth . . . I bought her in Richmond, Va., last Spring, a year ago, and she may have made an attempt to get back. I will give the above reward if she is caught in any adjoining State, or thirty dollars if she is caught in this state, and placed in jail, so I can get her. [Signed] D.G. Hughes.[36]

Sheriffs also used advertisements to notify enslavers of the capture of their human property. Sheriff J. Bates Jr. posted an ad announcing the apprehension of Sarah. "Committed to the Jail of Mobile County [Alabama] by John F. Everitt Esq., a Justice of the Peace . . . a Negro Woman who says her name is SARAH, and says she belongs to Howell Rose, of Montgomery County. The owner is hereby requested to come forward, prove property and pay charges, or she will be sold."[37]

Finding testimonies from women who survived incarceration in the South's jails is challenging. However, the account of Anthony Burns, an escaped slave from Virginia, provides valuable insight into the suffering faced by enslaved women prisoners. While in solitary confinement at Lumpkin's slave jail in Richmond, Virginia, Burns witnessed a woman being strip-searched.

Through a crevice in the floor, Burns could see the woman as she stood "stark naked in the presence of two men." One was an overseer employed by Lumpkin, and the other was "a person who had come to purchase a slave." The experience of watching the woman being strip-searched left Burns horror-struck. So did hearing her pleading and "sobbing" as the overseer made her undress; the buyer wanted to "see for himself whether she was well formed and sound in body."[38]

Strip searches were a routine part of the enslaved experience. They took place inside of slave jails, on plantations, on auction blocks, and anywhere else enslaved people were confined, exhibited, or sold. Unfortunately, these inspections continue in jails and prisons today. During intake, after visits, following work details, after church services, and following any transport off the facility or transfer to another location of confinement, guards carefully evaluate the hair, nasal passages, ears, mouths, breasts, and genitals of prisoners—treated as state property—in a manner reminiscent of the ways enslavers, overseers, slave traders, and potential buyers inspected the bodies of the enslaved.

Lumpkin's Jail, sometimes called "the Devil's half acre," was hell on earth for the enslaved people imprisoned there. It was a place of great suffering—an evil realm where thousands of enslaved women, men, and children experienced brutal punishment. Owned by the notorious trader Robert Lumpkin, the slave jail was the biggest private holding facility in Richmond, Virginia.

Lumpkin began his career as an itinerant trader before leading Richmond's interstate slave trade—the second largest in the United States after New Orleans. He spent his days "roaming over the country, and picking up a husband here, a wife there, a mother in one place, an alluring maiden in another."[39] He built his fortune by breaking up families and building bonds between strangers, by linking broken souls with iron chains and selling them down the river to the far Southern market.

On November 27, 1844, Lumpkin purchased a slave trading complex worth $6,000 on Wall Street in Richmond's Shockoe Bottom district, just a few blocks from where the Capitol sits today. The property rested in a secluded ravine, one hundred feet below the ground. A slave jail sat in the center of the compound. It was an imposing structure, "forty-one feet long and two stories in height, with a piazza on both stories," fortified with a "high close fence, the top of which was thickly set with iron spikes."[40] Bearing some features of a modern correctional facility—barred windows, chained gates, a yard for prisoners to exercise in, and barbed wire fences—Lumpkin's Jail looked like a cross between Chicago's Cook County Jail and a chicken coop.

The complex consisted of four buildings: a brick dwelling house (which served as the private residence of Robert Lumpkin), a guest house (where buyers, sellers, and their enslaved laborers sometimes stayed overnight), a kitchen, tavern, and a "slave pen" or jail. A makeshift cemetery also bordered the property. To this day, it holds the remains of those who died during their imprisonment. Their unmarked graves act as silent witnesses to the cruelties they faced.

Lumpkin's prisoners lived in a world covered in pain, darkness, and disease. They spent their days and nights in a filth-ridden, overcrowded concrete cell with no access to toilets, fresh air, or sunlight. Steel bars shielded the windows while death's shadow hovered over the bodies of the sick and injured.

The jail was a breeding ground for violence; punishment and torture flourished behind its walls. In the "whipping room," female and male prisoners endured brutal floggings at the hands of an overseer. He forced them, one by one, to lie face down on the ground with their hands and feet "stretched and fastened" to a pair of iron rings, while he struck them with a leather whip. He did not stop until blood streamed from their backs.[41]

Violence flowed from the whipping room into Robert Lumpkin's bedroom. In his private residence, next to the jail, a "fair-faced" girl named Mary and an unnamed "Black concubine" suffered sexual abuse. Mary was only eight years old when she was enslaved by Robert Lumpkin.[42] He was thirty-four. Their "relationship" began in a way typical of this period: he sexually abused her. In 1845, at the age of thirteen, Mary gave birth to her first child, a daughter. She named her Martha. By 1857, at the age of twenty-five, she had given birth to five children, two daughters and three sons. Lumpkin fathered them all.[43]

Mary spent her childhood, adolescence, and early adult years on the jail compound. She witnessed the traffic in human souls from Lumpkin's bedroom window. She saw children like herself caged like baby birds, their fragile wings crushed under the heavy weight of slavery. She heard the wails of broken-hearted men torn from their families forever and watched as helpless wives and mothers marched chained together by the ankles.

Between 1849 and 1850, approximately thirty-two enslaved women and twenty-seven girls of various ages, including infants, entered Lumpkin's Jail.[44] For days, weeks, and sometimes months, they crowded together in a dark, dingy room with rotting walls and floors glossed with human waste. The strong smell of mildew, feces, urine, and body odor hung in the damp air of the room and covered everything in it, reminiscent of the slave dungeons on the West African coast.

In November 1849, Arena's world came crumbling down like the decaying walls around her. Imprisoned for weeks with her four children, she mothered them behind bars. The double burden of being a mother who was both incarcerated and enslaved bore heavily on her. One can only imagine the misery she endured.

In the absence of historical records documenting her experience, questions remain about what Arena suffered. Was she ever taken to the whipping room where her skin was cracked and torn by the lash? Was she sexually abused by Lumpkin, the overseer, or overnight guests? Similar questions exist about her ability to survive. Where did Arena find comfort? In her children? In other incarcerated enslaved mothers who shared in her pain? Where did she store her tears? Did she hide them from the curious stares of her little ones, or allow them to fall like hailstones in her lap? Did she collapse under the heavy weight of oppression, or was she held together by hope?

As the day of her sale approached, Arena faced the uncertainty of her fate and the fate of her children. Would the family be sold together, in the same way they were purchased? Or would they be divided between five strangers? According to a jail ledger kept by Robert Lumpkin, his only business record known to survive, Arena and her children were sold to S. B. Jones for $1,600 and "sent South." Although they might have traveled together to the Deep South, we have no way of knowing if they remained together after being sold. It is likely that they did not. The same is true of other families that appear in Lumpkin's ledger: "Lucy + 2 children; Ginny + children; Frances + child; Henrietta + 2; Mary + child; Priscilla + 3 children; Susan + 2; and Frances + daughters."[45]

Mary, Robert Lumpkin's child concubine, could relate to the experience of being sold and separated from family. She could understand the pain felt by enslaved girls all over the plantation South, girls, like Diana, whose experiences mirrored her own. Diana, a young housemaid, was sold after defending herself against sexual abuse. Virginia Hayes Shepherd, a former slave, witnessed it all: "Old master Gaskins . . . use to send Diana to the barn to shell corn. Soon he would follow. Of course she fought him, but he wanted her and he had her . . . Once when Diana was successful in fighting him off, he bundled her up, put her in a cart, and took her to Norfolk, Virginia and put her on the auction block."[46]

As human property, enslaved women and girls had no legal protection from rape by white men. When an enslaver took "sexual possession" of their bodies, he was acting on his legal rights.[47] Every part of an enslaved person's body belonged to the enslaver. Since rape was viewed as a property crime, an enslaver could not be held accountable for violating a female slave.

Slaveholders held no parental responsibility for the children they sired.[48] But some enslavers, such as Robert Lumpkin, chose to assume paternity over their human property. Before the start of the Civil War, Lumpkin liberated his children and sent them to the free state of Pennsylvania to receive an education. He financed their futures with money made from selling other people's offspring. "The father [Robert Lumpkin]," wrote Charles Henry Corey, "fearing that some financial contingency might arise when these, his own beautiful daughters, might be sold into slavery to pay his debts [kept them in Pennsylvania] where they would be safe."[49]

Mary made a monumental sacrifice to ensure her children's safety. She stayed with Robert Lumpkin. Even after receiving her freedom, before the Civil War, she continued to live with him. In 1866, one year before his death, it appears that Robert Lumpkin married her and made her the heir to his estate. Mary Lumpkin inherited the jail complex, the blood-soaked whips, the tear-stained floors, the unmarked graves, and a lifetime's worth of painful memories.

After the war, Mary leased the property to Nathaniel Colver, an abolitionist Baptist minister, to use as a seminary for formerly enslaved people. What was once "the Devil's half acre" became "God's half acre."[50] It is now the site of Virginia Union University, a historically Black university.

Concubines, captives, and hired slaves lived and labored on Lumpkin's compound. Anne Mathews, a "mulatto woman," spent over three and a half years working as a domestic at the jail. Edward Mathews, her enslaver, hired her out to Robert Lumpkin in 1849. With no fields to plow or crops to harvest, it is likely that Anne worked as a cook, laundress, or household servant—or all three.

Slave hiring was widely practiced throughout the South. In this system, a hirer would lease an enslaved laborer or a group of enslaved laborers to perform work for a couple of months to a few years for a set amount of money. Hiring costs could range from $100 to $600 per year. In this way, enslavers generated profit from the labor of the enslaved without investing in the work itself.

In rural agricultural areas, hired enslaved women labored in the fields, growing cotton, wheat, tobacco, corn, rice, and sugarcane. In urban cities such as Baltimore, Charleston, New Orleans, Richmond, and Washington, DC, they primarily worked as domestic servants. Anne Mathews entered the thriving domestic workforce of Richmond, a city with one of the highest concentrations of hired enslaved people and free Black people in the South.[51]

As a hired enslaved person, Anne enjoyed special privileges. Her enslaver allowed her to keep a portion of the wages she earned by doing extra work. With these few nickels and dimes, she took periodic trips to Philadelphia; in 1848, she had "left there a child."[52]

Anne made several trips to the City of Brotherly Love with her enslaver's permission. Each visit carried the risk of arrest in Richmond, where any enslaved person traveling without a pass or free papers could easily be taken for a runaway.

In urban cities throughout the South, including Richmond, enslaved people had more mobility but faced increased surveillance. Slave patrollers—known among the enslaved as "paddyrollers"—monitored their every step. Slave patrols, formed by county courts and state militias, played a key role in "watching, catching, or beating" enslaved individuals who violated laws regulating their behavior and movement.[53] "Wandering" about the city without a travel pass or badge, or staying out beyond curfew, were among the numerous offenses that could result in an enslaved person being captured and whipped by a private white citizen.

In Richmond and other Virginia cities, constables also enforced punishments against the enslaved. Employed by local governments, they received payments for whipping and imprisoning enslaved individuals. "I am paid fifty cents for every negro I arrest, and fifty cents more if I flog him," Constable John Capheart of Norfolk, Virginia, said of his "good job." "I have flogged hundreds. I am often employed by private persons to pursue fugitive slaves."[54]

On Thanksgiving Day 1853, Anne's worst fears came true. She was arrested, though not for a crime typically associated with enslaved individuals: Anne had been wrongfully accused of "being free and remaining in the Commonwealth contrary to law."[55]

It was an unusual case of mistaken identity and a perplexing reality faced by some enslaved women living in the city. Anne, however, could never have anticipated becoming a victim of it. Being mistaken for an unregistered free person was a serious offense under an 1806 law that prohibited freed individuals from remaining in Virginia for more than one year without registering with the clerk of the court. Had Anne truly possessed the second-class freedom for which she was arrested and failed to reregister every three years, at a cost of twenty cents, she risked being jailed as a "runaway" and sold into slavery by the county sheriff for the benefit of the poor.[56]

After spending several days and nights behind bars for a freedom violation, Anne was taken to the Richmond mayor's court to answer the charges. Forbidden to testify on her own behalf, she relied on Edward Mathews, her enslaver, and Robert Lumpkin to prove her innocence. Her "freedom" rested on their ability to prove her enslaved status. In statements to the mayor, Mathews and Lumpkin insisted that Anne had committed no crime. The mayor agreed and released her into their custody and warned both men to "instruct the Police of the city to regard her [Anne] as a slave and see that she should not be allowed the privileges of a free woman."[57]

Jane Crow's injustice impacted every aspect of a Black woman's life in the antebellum South. This was particularly evident in the case of Anne Matthews: she was enslaved within the chattel slavery system and forced to work in a slave jail, while also being incarcerated in a city jail. Being both incarcerated and enslaved uniquely shaped the lives of enslaved women caught in the racially charged criminal legal system of the South. For free Black women, the reality of a restricted form of freedom—one that could be revoked with just one missed payment—was equally significant.

As long as slavery existed, the privileges of freedom could never be fully realized for a Black woman. Slave codes—restrictive laws designed to control and punish both enslaved and free Black individuals—and other race-based legislation increased their risk of incarceration and enslavement. Enslaved women like Anne Mathews often served time for "crimes" that only free Black women could legally commit while free Black women ended up behind bars or on the auction block for violating laws that targeted the enslaved.

Running away—or "stealing" oneself—was considered a "slave crime," yet both enslaved and free women paid the penalty for it. If a free Black woman could not prove her free status, she faced punishment as an enslaved "runaway," as in the case of Ellen Banister.

Like most working-class free Black women, Ellen experienced employment barriers and economic hardship. She labored long hours for low pay, likely as a domestic servant, cooking, cleaning, washing clothes, and caring for her employer's children while providing for her two sons as best as she could. But in the winter of 1841, Ellen's life fell apart like an overworn dishrag. She was arrested on the street for "want of her free papers," and four months later, she was "hired out at public auction" to Deputy Sergeant Francis Spraggins for $53.55—the amount of her unpaid jail fees.

Ellen entered a world where the lines between slavery and freedom did not exist. For two years and eight months, she worked side by side with enslaved people who never knew freedom and with free people who never knew slavery until they ended up at Spraggins's place. At least four enslaved people and ten "free colored persons" were hired out or sold to the sergeant into what I call "debt slavery."[58]

Debt slavery involves holding a person captive for unpaid fines, fees, or debts stemming from incarceration in jail. It often includes selling and purchasing a person's labor for profit. Judges, jailers, sheriffs, enslavers, and hirers worked together to facilitate this practice.

Ellen's incarceration and the debt slavery that followed left her sons with no parental support. With their mother away, the youngsters had to find a way to survive. Were they fortunate enough to receive social welfare or "poor relief" from the county? Were they forced to become apprentices for a white family? Did they live in a state of involuntary servitude like their mother? Or were they stolen by slave catchers and sold down South never to see her again? We will never know.

Freedom and slavery were bound together. Having free status did not guarantee one's right to citizenship or protection under the law. On the contrary, Southern legislatures created new laws that specifically targeted free Black people. These "Black Laws," which varied by state, denied free individuals the right to vote, to serve in public office, to preach, to gather in groups without supervision, to own firearms, to testify in court, to give evidence against a white person, and to have a trial by jury.

In many states, including Maryland, it was a crime to be free, Black, and poor. In 1796, the Maryland General Assembly passed "An Act Regarding Negroes" prohibiting any "free negro, mulatto, or other person" from "living idle, without any visible means of maintenance [employment], or going at large through such county without any visible means of subsistence [housing]." Persons arrested for vagrancy—the practice of traveling from place to place without any means of support or a residence—were required to pay a thirty-dollar bond or leave the state within five days; they were essentially deported. Those who could not afford to pay or move away were "taken up and carried before some judge or justice of the peace" and committed to the "common gaol [jail] of the county."[59] After twenty days, they were sold into slavery or released upon paying their jail fees.

When we reflect on the earliest days of America's founding, we find that the criminalization of Black freedom did not begin in 1865; it started during chattel slavery. Even before the Thirteenth Amendment to the US Constitution determined that slavery or involuntary servitude could be used as a "punishment for crime," local and state laws already allowed for free Black people to be incarcerated and enslaved for petty offenses: failure to exit a slave-holding state within a certain period after receiving one's freedom, entering a state that prohibited the migration of free Black people, failure to have a job or a place to live, being too poor to pay jail fees or taxes, or failure to prove one's free status resulted in the loss of freedom for thousands who could not afford its high cost.

A routine trip to the grocery store nearly cost Julia Blackwell her hard-earned freedom. When she left home at nine o'clock one evening, she hoped to return safely. As a free Black woman working as a domestic in Washington, DC, she was aware of the dangers lurking around every corner. She knew that slave hunters and policemen posed a threat to her safety, and she hoped to avoid them that night. But as soon as she walked out the door she was apprehended. "Two men came up to me, one of whom caught hold of me and shook me, threatening, if I made a noise, to choke me to death," Julia recalled. One of the men "said that he was going to take me to jail; that I was a runaway slave. I began to cry, and told him that I was a free woman, begging him all the while to let me go."[60]

Julia was taken to an interrogation room where she endured hours of relentless questioning. "Keese asked me where I was born, where my parents lived, and if I was a free woman. I told him that I was free. He

[Keese] then said it was a lie, that he knew my master, and that he had sold my brother Daniel," she recalled. "I again began to cry, and begged him for God's sake to let me go. He then gave me a Bible and told me that if I would swear that I was a slave he would set me free and would give me my free papers. I refused to swear, when he told me that I would have to go to jail."[61]

After failing to intimidate Julia into confessing to a "crime" she did not commit, the arresting officer "spoke to several men inside of the jail" about her. "I believe she tells the truth and is a free girl," said one of the men. In the end, Keese conceded Julia's claim of innocence and let her go. Around midnight, he released her onto the dark streets to walk back home.

Fifteen-year-old Lucy Briggs never made her way back home. On November 22, 1841, she was committed to the Richmond City Jail after a warrant was issued for her arrest. Her crime? Lack of possession of free papers and wandering "at large" in the city without them; she was regarded as a fugitive.

Lucy spent 155 days in jail. For every day she spent incarcerated, she acquired fees: thirty-eight cents per day to pay the cost of her support, and eighty-four cents for the jailer to "turn key twice"—once to lock her in, and once to let her out. He weaponized his keys like an overseer wielded his whip.

Nearly five months after her arrest, Lucy was "carried into Court" and "did prove her freedom." But she was not allowed to go free. The judge ordered that "Lucy Briggs shod be hired out so long as may pay hir jail fees [total: $59.38]."[62]

On April 25, 1842, Lucy left the cell block for the auction block. She was taken to the old slave market and "hired out . . . for the peried [period] of fifty nine years." Unlike a traditional slave sale, the sheriff served as the auctioneer and the judge as the slave trader. For every dollar she accumulated in jail debt, Lucy repaid with one year of her life.

A life sentence in the Louisiana State Penitentiary turned into a death sentence for Celeste, after she was found guilty of striking Eloise Lavergne, a white woman. The enslaved woman was "at least one hundred years of age," and unfit for hard labor. "Scarcely able to sit or stand," she spent her last days lying on the floor of a damp, dirty cell.[63]

In 1853, the Prison Board recommended that Celeste be pardoned and returned to her enslaver, concluding that "she, of course, can be of no value" and "if the State has paid the owners of said slave Celeste, that they be required to return it." She died in prison the same year.

Before 1865, very few Black women were incarcerated in Southern prisons. This was largely due to chattel slavery, which limited the number of enslaved individuals entering prisons, even though it contributed to their mass incarceration in jails. Despite this, the existence of slavery did not prevent Black women from being overrepresented in the female prison population. During the early to mid-nineteenth century, both free Black women and enslaved women were imprisoned more frequently than white women. This trend has continued for over two hundred years.

One of the best examples of the racial disparities between Black and white women's incarceration exists in Louisiana. Between 1835 and 1862, sixty-one women entered The Walls (the Louisiana State Penitentiary in Baton Rouge, Louisiana). Thirty-three were enslaved, five were free women, and twenty-three were white.[64] Unlike most Southern states, where the prison population was mostly white and male, 60 percent of Louisiana's female prisoners were Black.

Celeste was one of fifteen women incarcerated at the Louisiana State Penitentiary in 1853. The youngest, Phoebe, was seventeen; at just twelve years old she was given a life sentence for "wounding" her mistress. Like Celeste, she was sentenced to die in prison, even though her victim survived. And, as with Celeste, her age was not taken into consideration. The fact that the adult woman she allegedly wounded was, most likely, the aggressor was also ignored.

Phoebe and Celeste received excessive prison sentences for self-defense related "crimes." But this was not unusual. Almost every Black woman incarcerated at the Louisiana State Penitentiary was sentenced to life. In fact, the Louisiana State Penitentiary incarcerated more Black women with life sentences than any other prison in antebellum America.[65]

Some were convicted of murder. Others went to prison for arson, poisoning, attempted poisoning, and burglary, while a few ended up being "forfeited to the state." When an enslaved person entered prison, he or she automatically became state property, and the state was legally required to pay an enslaver the estimated value of the person. However, sometimes enslavers lost their human property through forfeiture, which by definition, means the loss of any property without compensation because of breach of a contractual obligation.

Children born to mothers in prison were also considered state property; by law, they inherited the status of their mother. On December 11, 1848, the Louisiana state legislature passed "An Act Providing for the disposal of such slaves as are or may be born in the Penitentiary." Under this act, an enslaved child born in prison would be sold at age ten. The Baton Rouge sheriff facilitated these cash-only sales, posting advertisements in newspapers and on courthouse doors. It was his role to ensure the highest bidder for the state.[66]

By the end of the Civil War, an estimated one million Black individuals had served time in jails and prisons across the Southern United States. Although the Thirteenth Amendment abolished chattel slavery and granted legal freedom to Black Americans in 1865, they continued to face the risk of being caught up in the criminal legal system or subjected to racially biased laws that undermined their freedom. As the nation underwent changes, the limitations on Black freedom grew tighter. Although Black people were no longer considered private property, they were not fully recognized as citizens either.

As the criminal legal system persisted in its enforcement of second-class freedom for Black women in the years immediately following Emancipation, unchecked racial violence showcased the harshest reality of freedom's aftermath. Becoming free sometimes cost Black women their lives.

The post–Civil War era represented a pivotal moment in American history, marked by the end of chattel slavery, the onset of freedom, and an increase in racial violence. Enslavers transformed into Grand Dragons, sheriffs into Klansmen, jailers into vigilantes, and police officers into lynch mobs. They used nooses and gavels, warrants and contracts, state and local laws, and the US Constitution to construct and enforce new boundaries on Black freedom. The battle over slavery may have ended in 1865, but the War on Black Freedom intensified.

CHAPTER 2

FREEDOM'S AFTERMATH

Most children start kindergarten at age five, but at that age, Harriet Purdy was already working as a slave. As an enslaved child, she likely spent her days around the Big House, gathering sticks for firewood, carrying pails of water, planting seeds, and caring for infants and toddlers. Her childhood was short and strenuous; little Black girls were barely potty trained before they began babysitting their enslavers' children.

By the time she reached adolescence and adulthood, these small jobs would have evolved into hard labor. While historical records do not specify the type of work Harriet performed, she may have served as a field hand, a house servant, a nanny, or even a wet nurse. If forced to work in the fields, she would have toiled for between ten and fourteen hours a day, cutting grass, clearing weeds, sowing crops, picking corn, threshing wheat, and curing tobacco. If forced to work in the Big House, she would have risen every morning at dawn to cook meals, boil laundry, empty chamber pots, and wash floors. And if forced to wet-nurse, Harriet would have spent part of her time breastfeeding a white child that in time would likely inherit her as property.

In 1865, the Thirteenth Amendment formally abolished slavery in the United States, giving Harriet legal ownership over her body, life, and labor. At last, she possessed the freedom to make her own choices—to decide what to wear, when to eat, when to sleep, who to love, where to live, and who to work for or not. She could pack up her tattered cotton dresses, head wraps, wooden-soled shoes, and any special mementos she may have cherished—a rag doll, a swath of clothing, a handmade quilt, a favorite barrette, or a lock of hair from a loved one—and leave the plantation behind. Harriet could walk hundreds of country miles in search of missing family members or catch a train to the city to look for a job. If she had "jumped the broom" during slavery and wanted to make her union legal, she could go to the county clerk's office and apply for a marriage certificate. If she and her husband managed to get "a little ole piece of money," as Bongy Jackson's parents did, she could have a "real weddin'." She could hire a Black preacher and dress up "like a bride an' all."[1]

Harriet savored the sweet taste of freedom, but not for long. The bitter realities of being a first-time citizen proved difficult to bear. She had no home, no job, no food, no education, and no money. There was no safety net waiting on the other side of slavery, just a tight web of lynch ropes, handcuffs, and anti-Black freedom laws.

This chapter explores how Black women navigated the challenges and dangers that arose in the aftermath of gaining their freedom. It chronicles their struggles to survive and defend their liberty against the persistent injustices of Jane Crow: racial violence, exploitative policing, race-based imprisonment, and racially biased laws that continued to threaten their freedom.

In her transition from slave to citizen, Harriet faced many of the same challenges that formerly incarcerated women experience today. She entered freedom with only the clothes on her back and an uncertain sense of identity. Although she was no longer legally enslaved, she was not completely free. She had no birth certificate to document her humanity; a bill of sale continued to define her existence.

Even after her enslavement ended, Harriet's forever freedom status remained conditional. As a Black woman, she possessed a second-class freedom that could be revoked at any time for breaking the law and thus the conditions of her liberty outlined in the Thirteenth Amendment. According to the amendment, if Harriet committed a crime, she could be re-enslaved by the criminal legal system as punishment. Her situation illustrated one of the most troubling aspects of Jane Crow's injustice: the increased risk of incarceration stemming from unequal freedom.

Harriet's unequal access to freedom not only heightened her susceptibility to incarceration but also made it difficult for her to integrate into society. She faced many of the same challenges that individuals encounter when returning home from prison today. Like Harriet, these "returning citizens"—individuals who have been recently released from incarceration—experience problems securing the basics: food, shelter, and employment. Their lack of citizenship, enshrined by the "black box," also holds them back from other essentials of freedom: the ability to vote, pursue an education, and reunite with lost loved ones. For Black women, these struggles are even greater. Their access to freedom and its benefits remains restricted by racism, just as it was in Harriet's time.

In March 1865, the United States Congress established the Bureau of Refugees, Freedmen, and Abandoned Lands, more commonly known as the Freedmen's Bureau. This federal agency aided formerly enslaved people like Harriet in the initial stages of their transition to freedom by addressing their immediate needs. Black community organizations, known as mutual aid societies, continued to assist newly freed people just as they had before the Civil War.

About a quarter of the country's four million former slaves received support from the Freedmen's Bureau. White bureau agents, who functioned as social workers, provided them with food, clothing, housing, legal aid, and healthcare. They also helped negotiate labor agreements with white landowners, reunited families separated during slavery, formalized marriages through civil ceremonies, and set up schools for those seeking education.

For as long as chattel slavery existed in the United States, Black people were legally barred from receiving an education. Southern legislatures instituted laws prohibiting enslaved people from learning to read or write and made it a crime for others to teach them. The ban on education for Black people created a racial literacy gap that exists to this day.

After the war, the Freedmen's Bureau began to invest in Black education by providing books and school buildings. Bureau agents served as superintendents of these schools, playing a crucial role in educating the formerly enslaved.[2] However, most of the support came from freed people themselves. They saved their pennies to hire teachers and purchase land. They built buildings with their calloused hands and turned old slave shacks, barns, and churches into makeshift classrooms.

Students of all ages crowded into these simple schoolhouses. It was not unusual to see groups of fifteen- and five-year-olds practicing spelling words together or elders, whose hands had grown arthritic from picking cotton, learning to trace the letters of the alphabet. Each generation understood that education and liberty were closely intertwined. But racial inequality made it difficult for new citizens to hold onto their freedom.

In freedom's aftermath, Southern state governments enacted a series of racially biased laws known as the Black Codes—which grew out of slave codes—to control formerly enslaved people and restrict their freedom. Freed people could not own firearms, vote, serve on juries, testify against a white person in court, speak loudly, spit in public, "play games" (gamble), lose their earnings, or be without a job. Nearly every aspect of their lives was criminalized and their citizenship denied.

In Mississippi, for example, breaking a labor contract or failing to provide proof of employment resulted in confinement in a county jail. In South Carolina, failing to purchase a license to work in an occupation other than servant or field hand amounted to a criminal offense. The penalty? A fine of $20 to $200.[3]

The Fourteenth Amendment, ratified in 1868, granted citizenship to "all persons born or naturalized in the United States," including the formerly enslaved. It constitutionally protected their civil rights, such as freedom of speech, a fair trial, freedom of religion, the legal right to work, and protection under US laws. But these rights were routinely denied, including the right to vote for Black men convicted of crimes.

The Fourteenth Amendment prohibited Black men with criminal convictions from voting, even before the Fifteenth Amendment formally granted voting rights.[4] Through a constitutional loophole, states had the power to refuse the franchise to anyone with "participation in rebellion or other crime." The same amendment that guaranteed the rights of formerly enslaved people also enabled widespread felony disenfranchisement.[5]

Lawmakers codified Black inequality at every level of government, hindering Black individuals from exercising their civil rights. However, racially biased laws were not the only barrier Black Americans faced in their perilous journey to equal citizenship. They confronted lynch mobs and vigilante terrorists as well.

Black women's journey to freedom and citizenship was characterized by extreme violence. Although the Fourteenth Amendment gave Black women a right to protection under the law, it did not shield them from lawless white men. When they exercised their freedom of speech, they were assaulted and sometimes killed. When they supported the political rights of their husbands, even though they could not vote themselves, they were strung up on trees and hanged right beside them. When they appeared in court to exercise their rights to a fair trial, they were subjected to all-white juries. When they practiced their right to worship, they had their churches burned to the ground.

Living as a Black woman in the Jane Crow South meant facing a constant threat of violence, often from those hired to protect them—the police. Unprovoked attacks occurred everywhere: at home, at work, in the woods, walking down city streets, strolling along country roads, standing on the sidewalk, riding the train, and laboring in the fields, as well as in carceral settings such as convict lease camps, chain gangs, and peonage farms. Nowhere was safe.

In 1866, a mob of white police officers and vigilantes carried out a three-day massacre in Memphis, Tennessee, killing forty-six Black people and wounding at least eighty others, including Lucy Smith. Lucy courageously testified to a federal investigator about the injuries she sustained. "My neck was swollen up the next day, and for two weeks I could not talk to anyone," she told the man. Then she mentioned other wounds she incurred on that tragic day, wounds that left her broken in places that time could not mend. "After the first man had connexion with me, another got hold of me and tried to violate me, but I was so bad that he did not," she recalled. "He gave a lick with his fist and said that I was so damned near dead he would not have anything to do with me," nor would the officers watching. "There were two policemen with the men," Lucy recalled. "I saw their stars."[6]

White men used the weapon of rape to terrorize and control Black women. They acted without fear of consequences, shielded from punishment in the same way that enslavers were. Historical records from this period show no cases in which a white assailant faced prosecution for assaulting a Black woman. The rape culture developed in chattel slavery carried on in freedom's aftermath, victimizing Black women and girls who had legal rights to their bodies but no judge or jury willing to enforce them.

While Black mothers and fathers taught their children how to survive, some white men were instructing their sons in the ways of violence. They taught their boys to tie lynch ropes before they learned to tie their shoes, to sexually profile Black girls before puberty, and to hate "n——s" before they even understood the word's meaning. "I have seen very small white children hang their Black dolls," one woman remembered. However, she did not fault them for their actions. She reasoned, "It is not the child's fault, he is simply an apt pupil."[7]

As these innocent boys developed into fully grown racist men, they stopped playing make-believe and started leading lynch mobs. During the first nadir of American race relations (1865–1965), a period when racism was more overt and widespread than in any other time in the nation's history, white supremacist groups such as the Ku Klux Klan (KKK) unleashed a long reign of terror in the South. However, this epidemic of racial violence spread across the entire United States. Everywhere Black people traveled, a noose was sure to follow.

On May 2, 1911, in the rural, predominately white town of Okemah, Oklahoma, Laura Nelson had her first and last run-in with the law. She was home alone with her children when Deputy Sheriff George Loney and a posse of three white men showed up on her doorstep. They came in search of a missing cow. Laura claimed to know nothing about it.

Days earlier, Laura's husband, Austin, had stolen the animal and butchered it. His family lived hand to mouth, and he had nothing for his children to eat. For this act of survival, a judge sentenced him to three years in the Oklahoma State Penitentiary.[8]

Saving his children's lives cost Austin his freedom. But Laura paid the biggest price for his "crime." Sheriff Loney found a firearm while searching the family's property, a discovery that could have easily resulted in Laura's death. But Lawrence, the Nelsons' fourteen-year-old son, grabbed the family rifle when Loney tried to seize it, firing a lethal shot into the sheriff's hip that traveled to his abdomen.

Laura and Lawrence were both arrested and charged with murder. Laura pleaded their innocence, explaining to authorities that it was an accident. But her cries for mercy fell on deaf ears. Desperate and afraid, Laura did the only thing she could to get free: she tried to "throw herself out a window" at the Okfuskee County Jail.[9]

Laura knew she would not survive as a marked woman. It was not uncommon for lynch mobs to capture Black people from jails, courtrooms, and police custody. And it was not unusual for correctional officers and policemen to participate in these crimes. Laura felt it best to end her own life to avoid being hanged or dying in prison. But she did not succeed in exiting the world on her terms.

At around midnight on May 25, one day before their scheduled arraignment, a mob looked for Laura and Lawrence at the jail. The boy was asleep in his bunk when "a dozen to forty men" stormed in and took hold of him. Next, they went searching for Laura. She could hear their heavy boots clopping against the cement floor like a herd of wild horses. The time had finally come for her to die. In the early hours of the morning, Laura was taken to an all-Black town and lynched from a railroad bridge over the North Canadian River. Lawrence was hanged there, too, twenty feet from his mother.[10]

The gruesome scene drew an audience of fifty-eight spectators—thirty-five men, six women, and seventeen children. All of them white. They came to take in the sight: to watch the listless bodies blowing in the gentle wind, their heads drooping like weeping willow branches, with tears streaming from their eyes.

The "lynching party" ended at around eleven o'clock in the morning when Laura and Lawrence were cut down by order of the county commissioners. A horse-drawn wagon carried their bodies back to Okemah, where they were buried in two unmarked graves—but never truly laid to rest. To this day, their family has received no justice for their murders.

Black people in America are still waiting for justice. As I write this book, the world is witnessing the historic conviction of former Minnesota police officer Derek Chauvin for the murder of George Floyd. On May 25, 2020, exactly 109 years to the day Laura and Lawrence Nelson were hanged, Chauvin pressed his knee into the neck of a Black man he was sworn to "protect and serve," choking the life out of him. Three other officers observed and participated in what many see as a modern-day lynching.

Lynch mobs still exist in the twenty-first century. They hide behind blue suits and badges instead of in white robes and hoods, and they carry Glock 19s instead of nooses. They openly document their crimes on body-worn cameras, creating a visual record of racial violence eerily similar to what we see in lynching photographs. The only difference between lynching then and now is that Black families go to morgues to collect their slain loved ones rather than cutting them down from trees, telephone poles, or timber bridges.[11]

Following the Civil War, thousands of freedwomen fled the countryside to escape racial violence and secure better economic opportunities. They relocated to cities, filling up shacks and run-down apartment buildings in the poorest, most segregated sections of the urban South. Some found low-wage jobs as cooks, washerwomen, and general house servants for white families. Others found no employment at all.

After the war, working for "white folks [was] just as bad as, if not worse than it was during the days of slavery," one woman recalled. "Tho' today we are enjoying nominal freedom, we are literally slaves."[12] Day and night, this woman served at the beck and call of her "mistress." Whenever she sat to eat, laid down to rest, or knelt to pray, she could expect to hear "'Mammy, do this,' or 'Mammy, do that.'" The exhaustion, isolation, and oppression weighed her down like a two-ton anchor. "I am not permitted to rest . . . I don't know what it is to go to church; I don't know what it is to go to a lecture or entertainment or anything of the kind; I live a treadmill life and I see my own children only when they happen to see me on the streets when I am out with the children [of her 'mistress']," she lamented.[13]

Aware of the challenges faced by house servants, some Black women opted to work independently as laundresses. This occupation allowed them to remain close to their children and distant from white control. But laundry work was the most challenging—and underpaid—domestic job. The average worker earned between four and eight dollars per week. Even so, washerwomen enjoyed a level of independence that house servants did not. They worked from the comfort of their own homes, shielding themselves from physical and sexual violence and other hidden dangers present in the households of white employers. They also set the terms of their employment, deciding how many hours they would work and how much they would earn.[14]

Hard work is what kept Black women and their children alive. To secure a roof over their heads and food on the table meant scrubbing on a washboard until their knuckles turned pink and raw. It meant wringing clothes until their fingers and palms shriveled up like prunes, then hanging laundry until their shoulder muscles burned like hot coals. It meant using whatever strength they had left to iron and fold the laundry before lugging it back to the homes of their clients.

Domestic workers in white households faced equally grueling labor and low pay. To make up for what they lacked in wages, some resorted to stealing. Stealing food became an important act of survival. Servants took whatever they could—leftover ham, eggs, cornbread, and other "vittles and fixin's"—to feed themselves and their children. However, this practice, often referred to as "pan-toting," involved significant risk. The penalty for taking anything from a white person's table varied widely based on the employer's mood. Some supervisors overlooked missing scraps, while others reported them stolen. Accusations of property theft—including food—landed more Black women in jail than any other "crime."

When Harriet Purdy left her childhood home—the plantation—she traveled to Annapolis, Maryland, hoping to start a new life. If she was fortunate, she might find work as a house servant or washerwoman. At least then, she thought, she would not have to worry about being drawn back into the fields or sold into slavery. In 1866, she was arrested for allegedly stealing a pair of white lady's alligator boots.[15]

Black women were often arrested for taking things they never touched. Still, one can imagine the desperate circumstances that might have led Harriet to steal. She had trouble pulling herself up by her bootstraps, especially since she had no boots. Taking those "gaiter" boots could have literally and figuratively helped her get on her feet after slavery.

At the October 1866 term of the Anne Arundel County Circuit Court, Harriet was convicted of "petit-larceny," a small-scale property crime, and sentenced "to be sold for a term of one year in the State."[16] Notice of the "public sale" was posted in the *Annapolis Gazette*. Similar announcements for the sale of freed people appeared in the advertisements section of local newspapers, on the doors of county courthouses, and in public places all over the South.

In Maryland, post-Emancipation slave sales took place at the Anne Arundel County courthouse. The federal-style building resembled a slave pen with its simple rectangular shape and brick wall enclosure. Its front roof gave the "appearance of wings," though there was nothing holy or sacred about this place.[17] The courthouse is where Black people were sold like livestock, sentenced to incarceration, and legally lynched on the gallows.

Courthouses have long been sites of oppression and resistance for Black Americans. In courtrooms all over the country, Black women, men, and youth have faced the most extreme punishments for the pettiest of "crimes," often with the least protection of their legal rights. The sentencing of a Black woman named Geneva Cooley to life without parole for a nonviolent drug charge is a striking example. Or the locking away of Curtis Wilkerson for life for stealing a pair of white tube socks worth $2.50.[18]

In addition to punishing Black people more often and more severely than whites, the criminal legal system continues to disproportionately violate the constitutional rights of Black citizens by failing to ensure a "speedy and public trial by an impartial jury." All-white juries remain the norm in many jurisdictions, and case delays result in Black people spending more time in confinement, with higher bail amounts.[19]

These modern violations of the Sixth Amendment to the US Constitution echo the actions of Southern judges who refused to acknowledge the Civil Rights Act of 1866—America's first civil rights law, which granted fundamental citizenship rights to all individuals born in the United States. The act was later replaced by the Fourteenth Amendment.

Judge Daniel Magruder of Anne Arundel County violated Harriet Purdy's civil rights when he denied her the chance to testify at her trial. But her testimony would not have changed the outcome. The all-white jury had already decided her guilt before Magruder raised his gavel.

Standing outside the courthouse, Harriet must have felt the cold December air cutting through her dress. She did not have a blanket to shield her from the wind, nor a just legal system to protect her from losing her freedom. The same laws that authorized free Black Marylanders to be sold as a punishment for crimes during the early nineteenth century were used to sentence Harriet, a freedwoman, several decades later.

Elijah L. Rockhold, a former enslaver, purchased Harriet for thirty-four dollars, and for one year, she worked on his farm.[20] Nothing could have prepared her for the experience of returning to slavery—or of enduring its exploitation again, this time as a freedwoman. She must have wondered, *What good is liberty if one can quickly lose it? How can a person be free yet still susceptible to slavery?* Harriet's status remained unclear, like many formerly incarcerated Americans today. She was not a chattel slave, but she was also not a full citizen. Harriet could no longer be held as private property but she could be treated—and sold—as public property. The Thirteenth Amendment protected her from a lifetime of slavery. Still, it allowed her to be re-enslaved as a punishment for crime.[21]

CHAPTER 3

DEBT SLAVERY

"Oh, yes, oh, yes," Sheriff William Lawson exclaimed from the podium. "How much am I offered to start the negro?" Buyers gathered around the auction block, ready to cast their bids. A large crowd assembled to watch.

The novelty of a slave sale taking place in 1902 sparked doubts among suspicious buyers. As they circled around the auction block, they openly questioned their rights to the property being sold, especially since the auction was taking place thirty-seven years after the end of chattel slavery. However, Sheriff Lawson settled their fears, reassuring them that the individuals were "criminals" who, by law, could be sold into slavery.

Clara Anderson and Belle Griffin stood anxiously as the men cast their bids. Neither could not have imagined that a simple charge of vagrancy would turn into a slave auction, and that they would be the ones being put up on the block. But Jane Crow's injustice demanded it.

Under normal circumstances, a "crime" of vagrancy would have been punished with a small fine or a thirty-day sentence in the Lancaster County Jail. But Clara and Belle were Black women who lacked the protections typically associated with whiteness. The judge set their bail at one hundred dollars—about six month's wages for a washerwoman or domestic servant.

With barely enough money to buy a bag of cornmeal, the women could not afford to pay their bail in cash. Even if they somehow managed to gather the funds, it would have bought only temporary freedom. They would still have to endure the judge's harsh ruling—being "put up on the block" and auctioned off "to the highest bidder."[1]

Even though the Thirteenth Amendment formally abolished slavery in the United States, Black women and men still faced the threat of being sold on the auction block. It may be surprising to learn that these sales were entirely legal after the Civil War and persisted into the twentieth century. They were advertised in local newspapers and carried out in former slave markets, public squares, and on the grounds of county courthouses. Sheriffs—and sometimes judges—conducted these auctions just as they had before the war.

The stories in this chapter are crucial for understanding how mass incarceration evolved after the Civil War, transitioning from a system designed to protect slavery to one used to perpetuate it. From the experiences of Black women, we learn how jails fostered this rising trend in punishment, turning poverty and debt into crimes punishable by slavery.

This chapter traces the experiences of Black women trapped in debt slavery since 1865. It follows their journey from being sold into fixed-term slavery to being hired out to private peonage farms. It also chronicles their forced labor on chain gangs and their confinement due to cash bail.

After the abolition of chattel slavery, Black women continued to endure mass jailing and enslavement for nonviolent "crimes." Some were sold for petty theft or unpaid fines; others were sold for vagrancy. Despite the differences in the "crimes" that landed Black women on the auction block or in a holding cell—where they waited until a court sold their labor to a white landowner—they all shared one experience: these women were victims of a criminal legal system that punished them for being free, Black, and poor.

Vagrancy—defined as living without a home, regular employment, or income, or traveling without working—had a significant impact on Black women. Each day, they faced the criminal legal system's scrutiny over their ability to provide for themselves. Demonstrating income became akin to having a certificate of freedom. When they couldn't produce such evidence, they risked arrest, fines, or being sold into slavery.

After 1865, more Black women were sentenced to fixed-term slavery for vagrancy than for any other "crime." I use the term *fixed-term slavery* to describe the auctioning and selling of Black citizens into temporary enslavement. Unlike chattel slavery, this system had a specified end date, and the status of a fixed-term enslaved person could not be inherited.

In Maryland, freedwomen such as Harriet Purdy were subjected to the same vagrancy laws as free Black women in the pre–Civil War South. These laws, which persisted through chattel slavery and Jane Crow, imposed the harshest penalty on Black women who violated them: a sentence of fixed-term slavery. But very few whites endured this extreme punishment from the courts, and when a judge did sentence a white person to slavery, it was only for a short period. The penalty for being poor and white was a month or two of servitude; being Black and destitute meant spending many months or even years in bondage.

At times, jailers saved white prisoners from being sold at auctions. One such instance occurred in Brooksville, Kentucky, when Jailer Metcalfe liberated Henry Dodson in 1887. Dodson, a "chronic vagrant," had been arrested and imprisoned multiple times. During his last arrest, he had requested an immediate trial to avoid waiting in jail. The judge granted Dodson's request but handed down an unexpected sentence: "his services sold for the period of seventy-five days."[2]

Standing before the courthouse doors, the sheriff "seemed to feel his position much more keenly than did Dodson." He never imagined "knocking down" another white man or negotiating his labor like that of an enslaved person. Shame landed on him like an auction hammer hitting a sound block without warning.

The sale moved slowly—like Black progress after Emancipation—until Jailer Metcalfe stepped in. He announced to the "large crowds" that "he could not bear to see a white man in slavery." Then he pulled a dollar from his pocket and purchased Dodson's freedom.[3]

Vagrancy laws were enforced with a clear racial bias. While poor white men were punished for breaking these laws, their treatment was less severe than that of Black women and men. White women, on the other hand, were not subject to these laws; in most states, vagrancy statutes applied to women only if they were Black.

Belle Griffin and Clara Anderson experienced the full weight of the vagrancy law when they came under Sheriff Lawson's hammer. Belle "brought $5" and was "sold for 12 months." Clara was "knocked down" for five dollars and sold for three years, though according to Kentucky law, her sentence should not have exceeded twelve months.[4]

The courts played a crucial role in sustaining fixed-term slavery. The power to decide who would be "bound out to labor or sold into servitude" rested in the hands of all-white juries and judges. As a result, disproportionate numbers of Black citizens were convicted, imprisoned, and enslaved.[5]

When the court sentenced an individual to be sold as a slave, county sheriffs prepared broadsides to advertise the sale.[6] These posters, modeled after early nineteenth-century slave sale advertisements, contained detailed descriptions of Black prisoners and the crimes they were accused of. Additionally, they listed the auction date, time, and location; the name and age of those being sold; the length of time the sheriff was selling them for; and the term of purchase, which was cash.

Once a person became a fixed-term slave, they lost their right to freedom. It was a crime for them to leave the state or "unlawfully depart" from the service of their "masters." They were legally bound until their sentence expired or a judge freed them. If they escaped, any county court judge could issue a warrant for their arrest and have them brought before the bench. If the judge found the claims against the accused "runaway" valid, the individual would be returned to their enslaver or committed to the county jail.

It is essential to understand that fixed-term slaveholders did not have the same rights as antebellum enslavers. They could not hold human beings in bondage for life, sell or inherit them as property, or transfer them to another owner. They could not take out insurance policies on their lives. After Emancipation, as Black people ceased to be privately held property, the market value of Black life declined, making such policies unnecessary to obtain. Unlike those enslaved under chattel slavery, fixed-term enslaved people had no market value; enslavers extracted profit solely from their labor, not from their status as property.

Newspaper analysis reveals that fixed-term slaveholders paid between twenty-five cents and thirty-seven dollars to purchase Black women's labor. In Maryland, where post-Emancipation slave sales seemed to occur regularly, women were "sold for an average price of about $30," a high rate for an enslaved citizen. Still, as one observer remarked, it was much "cheaper to buy slaves under the present laws of the South than it was formerly to purchase them."[7] In the antebellum slave market, these women would have sold for more than seventeen times the price.

The criminal legal system placed a high value on Black women even though their smaller numbers and price, compared to Black men, do not reflect this. To understand the worth assigned to Black women's work, one must look at sentencing patterns. These patterns reveal that judges sentenced fewer Black women to fixed-term slavery—but for longer terms than men.

Courts punished Black women more harshly and extracted more labor from them, as evidenced by their lengthy sentences. This unequal treatment is apparent in the case of Clara and Belle, who were sentenced to one and three years, respectively, for the "crime" of vagrancy, while William A. Reed, accused of the same offense and auctioned alongside them, received only three months of slavery.

In Maryland, Dilly Harris was sentenced to two years of slavery for stealing. Gassaway Price was auctioned for the same crime and sold for one year. Both individuals were described as "aged about Thirty years," which suggests they would have been in their prime and capable of ordinary labor. Yet prospective buyers valued the man more: Gassaway was "knocked down" for thirty-five dollars. Dilly went for twenty-five dollars. In most cases, men sold for higher prices than women.[8]

At an auction site in Richmond, Kentucky, three prisoners—two men and one woman—were "put up and sold to the highest bidder" for violating the state vagrancy law. One man was sold for thirty-eight dollars and sentenced to twelve months of slavery. The second man sold for fourteen dollars and three months. But the woman received the lowest bid—twenty-five cents for twelve months of bondage.[9]

The cost of Black women's lives declined by over 90 percent in 1865. But the exploitation of their labor continued to rise. Kentucky and Maryland were just two of several states to legalize fixed-term slavery. Sheriffs auctioned Black citizens to private landowners in the Upper South, Deep South, and border states, including Missouri.

On April 23, 1892, Sheriff Creiger marched Mary Whiteside, Henry Thompson, William Miller, and John Wilkins into the public square and sold them "into sixty days' slavery."[10] Their "crime"? Failing to provide a visible means of support. Mary was "put up first on the block." She brought ten dollars for the sixty days' work the county fined her. After paying costs—or what I call "freedom fees"—the court applied the money from her sale to her debts under Missouri's vagrancy law.

Jane Crow's inequality limited Mary's employment opportunities. She may have been unable to find a job or temporarily unemployed at the time of her arrest. Instead of receiving compassion, she was labeled a "criminal" and a slave. Her story exposes the immorality of a system that profited from a Black woman's labor instead of allowing her the grace to be poor.

Just days before the Missouri Supreme Court established the precedent of "once free, always free" in the slave freedom suit *Winny v. Whitesides*, the practice of selling Black "vagrants" was written into law. In 1818, Winny, an enslaved woman, sued for her freedom, claiming that her enslaver,

Phebe Whitesides, had unlawfully enslaved her.[11] On December 30, 1824, the Missouri Supreme Court officially granted Winny her freedom. Yet those subjected to the state's vagrancy law remained in bondage, despite being legally free.

More than seventy years after the landmark *Winny v. Whitesides* ruling, and well into the 1900s, Missouri continued to sentence Black women and men to slavery. The state vagrancy law prevailed over the abolition clause of the Thirteenth Amendment, leaving formerly enslaved citizens and their descendants vulnerable to arrest, incarceration, and sale. The same was true in the Deep South, where judges and magistrates used these laws, along with the Thirteenth Amendment exception clause, to enslave Black Americans through the criminal legal system.

Since Emancipation, the criminal legal system has perpetuated slavery. Its roots can be traced to the domestic slave trading era of the nineteenth century, and its branches extend to the intraregional exchange of Black prisoners after the Civil War. Between 1865 and 1945, more than eight hundred thousand Black women, men, and youth were trafficked through a third forced migration, which I call the "post-Emancipation prisoner trade."[12] This term describes the commercial transport of incarcerated people for profit to white landowners, private companies, and public chain gangs.

In the South, plantation owners, lessees, and chain gang bosses served as the primary exploiters of unfree labor, while state and local penal and judicial systems supplied them with laborers. In this way, criminal legal authorities acted as traders, facilitating the sale and transportation of incarcerated people across the city limits and county lines throughout the Upper and Deep South.

The post-Emancipation prisoner trade carried people hundreds of miles away from family, friends, and the lives they had begun to build after slavery. On roads in Virginia, North Carolina, South Carolina, Georgia, Alabama, Florida, Arkansas, Louisiana, Mississippi, or Texas, it was not unusual to see a Black woman or man being hauled in a wagon in chains. These voyages sometimes lasted a week or longer and ended at plantations, prison factories, or public roads, where incarcerated people were delivered like cargo. One is left to wonder about the fate of those who did not survive the trips.

The journey from freedom to bondage often began in a courtroom. Although rarely identified as perpetrators, judges and all-white juries played an important role in facilitating the re-enslavement of Black Americans after the Civil War. Through mass convictions and long sentences, they supplied an involuntary labor force, forcing generations of Black people into unpaid work for private and public industries.

Local sheriffs colluded with judges, which was key in keeping the trade alive. These elected officials served as brokers, responsible for selling Black citizens into debt slavery. They also facilitated the auction of individuals sentenced to fixed-term slavery, employing the same strategies used by domestic slave traders. One strategy was auctioning individuals one at a time; another was selling people in "lots" at a reduced price.

Unfortunately, historical records from this period provide far less detail about Black women sold into fixed-term slavery than about men. Scholars must rely on accounts of male victims and descriptions of their auction block experiences to imagine what Black women endured. A well-documented auction in Bedford County, Virginia, offers some insight into what Black women likely faced.

On December 20, 1880, the sheriff of Bedford County, Virginia, "put up" three men for public sale. Standing behind a large wooden podium with a pistol, he appealed to the crowd for offers. "Remember, gentleman, you get these men for three months," he shouted. A handful of potential buyers hovered around the auction block to inspect the "lot" more closely. They thumped the men's chests, "examined their eyes and teeth," and "criticised them," one observer recalled.[13]

The scene was strange yet familiar, mimicking the sights and sounds of a traditional slave auction. The difference with this recent sale is that the sheriff did not prepare the men for the market as a seller usually would. He did not comb their hair or try to wash away the sullen expression from their faces. He did not lather their skin with pork fat to make it look "slick and lively." And no women were "put up" on the block with the men.

When sold at auction, a man or woman endured four centuries of oppression in just a few hours. They were taken from jail and delivered to the public square or courthouse. Sometimes they marched on foot. Other times, the sheriff transported them in a horse-drawn wagon. They wore the indignity like the dirty clothes on their bodies; incarcerated people often languished in jail for months until a magistrate ordered their sale.

As formerly enslaved citizens stood on the auction block, they could feel their freedom slipping away and the heavy chains of slavery returning. With them came the familiar taste of white men's dirty fingertips and the pain of brutal insults and racial epithets. One can only imagine the sense of powerlessness as they endured the shame of being reduced from citizens to commodities.

The eldest victim of the Bedford auction, "while not in his prime," was still considered able to "earn his own bread." Under the chattel slavery system, this "gray-haired old fellow" would have been classified as a quarter hand. Another man was "somewhat past middle age" and "feeble." Enslavers would have ranked him as a zero hand. The strongest man in the group was "well-developed [muscular]" and "able to perform any ordinary manual labor." He would have been valued as a "prime hand" or "first-rate slave."[14]

The sale attracted a large crowd, but the bidding was slow. Potential buyers placed little value on two of the men due to their advanced age and inability to perform strenuous labor. Frustrated and desperate, the sheriff reminded them that the "piece" was worth more than they were offering: "I am only offered the paltry sum of $1.50; too cheap." Ultimately, John Scott and Daniel Early purchased the men for four dollars, the highest bid received for their labor.[15]

The resurrected auction block haunted these men and every formerly enslaved person who gathered to watch the sale. They had witnessed families broken apart and sold, and many had stood on these wooden platforms themselves. Now, they were forced to relive the dreadful experience. "Dey gwine sell us all into slavery again" was a fear expressed by those dreading a return to chattel slavery.

However, Bedford's Black residents turned their fear into action, challenging the legality of the auction. They hired Henry C. Lowry, a prominent white attorney and member of the Virginia House of Delegates, to appeal the magistrate's decision. The circuit court judge, however, would not grant the appeal because the jurisdiction ceased with the magistrate's court.

Lowry sued out a writ of habeas corpus, which was made returnable before the county court. After reexamining the case, the judge ordered the three men discharged, ruling that their alleged "crime" did not fall under any of the "five heads of vagrancy" provided for by the statute and noting that the charge was not made by the overseer of the poor, as required by law. But the degradation of their experience could not be erased like their record. The abuse "cruelly brought their minds to the days of slavery," days they thought they had left behind.

Life at Turner's plantation vividly recalled the dark days of slavery. Tucked away in Tallapoosa County, Alabama, the plantation was where Black women and men arrested for petty "crimes" labored under the whip's sting. Sarah Nealy was one of them.

In 1903, Sarah, described as a "colored girl," was convicted on a trumped-up charge and sold to James Fletcher Turner, a wealthy cotton planter. On his plantation, she endured a fate similar to many Black women exploited as debt slaves. Only she was not enslaved for a fixed term; she was sold into a system known as peonage, where one-year contracts could last for decades as landowners refused to release workers until they paid their alleged debts.[16]

The peonage system thrived in the Deep South. It involved holding persons against their will and forcing them to work under the pretext of paying off a debt or criminal fine. However, the terms of a person's service rarely ended when they were supposed to. Through this system, individuals like Turner continued the practice of enslaving Black prisoners, sometimes for life.

Peonage, like fixed-term slavery, was driven by poverty and racially biased incarceration practices. Those who were convicted of a misdemeanor "crime" could be fined and then sent to work on a plantation until their debts were repaid. Through these unpaid debts, the court system created a pool of involuntary laborers for white landowners, supplying a low-cost workforce that they could easily exploit.

Police officers were central to enforcing these corrupt and abusive peonage practices. In the War on Black Freedom, these foot soldiers rounded up Black women and men for minor crimes or fabricated charges by the thousands. Faced with massive fines and court costs, many had no choice but to labor for a local employer who would pay their fees in exchange for their freedom.

Plantation owners hired agents to look for prospective peons. They searched small-town courtrooms for desperate people with no money to pay their penalties. Preying on their circumstances, brokers encouraged Black defendants to plead guilty, promising that they would pay their fines. Individuals then signed contracts with farm owners to settle the debts and avoid imprisonment. But charges—like clothing and food—continued to multiply on their accounts. By the time one debt was paid, another had accumulated.

While most planters acquired Black labor directly from the courthouse, James Fletcher Turner purchased his "stock" from both the courts and the police. J. F. Dunbar, a "night marshal," supplied him with debt slaves. Dunbar would, in his own words, "arrest the negroes after the trial" and transport them thirty miles from Goodwater to Dadeville, Alabama, "tied with ropes." Hoping for a higher profit, he sought out Turner as a buyer:

> "What are they worth?" asked Turner during one of their transactions.
>
> "$50," Dunbar answered.
>
> "I don't want them; too much," Turner replied.

"$46," Dunbar responded.

"No; too much," Turner fired back.

After intense haggling, Dunbar finally agreed to accept forty dollars for each prisoner.[17]

When the horse-drawn wagon pulled up to Turner's place, Sarah was met by the weary, curious stares of the men already there. Their eyes told a story of cold-blooded cruelty and "crimes that would disgrace and stain the darkest pages of the history of slavery."[18] Their bodies, weighed down by thick sores and heavy mud, told a similar tale of brutality and oppression.

The moment her feet hit the "new ground," Allen Turner, James Fletcher Turner's overseer and son, put Sarah to work. He ordered her to clear the land for farming and stack the brush in the fields. The work was physically demanding, and she struggled to keep up with the men. As a result, the overseer decided to make an example of her.

Sarah took off her clothes and lay naked across a tree trunk at Allen's command. Two men held her down while he "whipped her with a buggy trace 100 lashes."[19] He skinned Sarah's back with the same leather straps that drew the horse and wagon.

Allen "hit her a lick and then another in the same place nearly every time, raising blisters or drawing blood," recalled one witness. "He then put a pair of [hand]cuffs on her . . . and tied a rope around her wrists . . . and let her hang [over the limb of a tree] . . . Just about dinner we lowered her down . . . Mr. Turner told me to throw her a pone of bread. She said she could not eat. Then Mr. Turner told me to throw the pone of bread to the dogs," the man continued.[20]

Allen forced him to go and tell Sarah she must return to work. But Sarah could not find her way to the fields. She "pulled the lid of her eye down and said she could not see."[21] She had been beaten so severely that her eyes had swollen shut.

No amount of salve, cloth strips, saltwater, or home remedies could restore Sarah's ability to work. She "crawled behind some bushes" and laid down instead. In the background, she could hear the bloodhounds smacking on her uneaten cornbread as if taunting her and Allen's footsteps tearing through the grass. She could feel the heat from his burning rage as he drew closer, followed by a blast of cold steel striking against her skull.

"Boss, she's dead," one of the witnesses cried out from the bushes. Allen ordered two of the six men to take Sarah's body to the nearby "Negro church" and dispose of it after dark. James Turner—the plantation owner—threatened to kill all of them if they ever told a soul.

"Somebody provided a rude box or coffin to bury her in," one pallbearer testified. Walking side by side, the men carried Sarah through the pitch-black woods for miles. When they arrived at the churchyard, they dug a grave and lowered her in. Today, this burial site still holds Sarah's remains and evidence of Allen Turner's crime. He was never charged with her murder.[22]

Several other Black women fell victim to Allen's rage. In 1902, Cornelia Hammock was convicted of larceny and sold to James Fletcher Turner to pay her fines and court fees, totaling $16.40. Just two days later, she died. Sarah Oliver's life ended just as quickly at Turner's place. Allen murdered her too.[23]

It is possible that Allen killed Cornelia, Sarah Oliver, and Sarah Nealy for personal reasons, such as resisting sexual advances. Rape was a defining feature of debt slavery, and overseers routinely abused Black women. While countless reports of sexual violence appear in historical records, Douglas A. Blackmon's research on the re-enslavement of Black Americans after the Civil War exposes the prevalence of such abuses on Turner's plantation. He writes, "The Turner farm was particularly notorious for sadistic inflictions upon sexually defiant Black women."[24]

Some victims ran away to escape the threat of death. Fearing for her life, Hazel Slaughter took flight after witnessing Allen beat a Black male prisoner to death. By the time the guards caught up with her, the dogs had torn her clothes and flesh apart.[25]

Decades after the ratification of the Thirteenth Amendment, Black women were still running for their lives and seeking freedom. They traveled through muddy rivers, snake-infested swamps, forests, and fields until they found safety. But many never did. Hundreds, if not thousands, were captured, jailed as "runaways," and returned to their enslavers.

Laborers called him "Massa Jim," though he did not begin enslaving human beings until after 1865. His father, Zadok Smith, taught him as a child how to turn people into commodities for profit, a skill he excelled at in his later years. By the dawn of the twentieth century, James Monroe Smith possessed more land, peons, and prisoners than any other landowner in Georgia and perhaps the entire United States.[26]

Smith, a millionaire planter and former senator from Georgia, rented hundreds of Black prisoners from the state and county to build his agricultural empire, known as Smithsonia. The plantation was enormous, covering thirty square miles and twelve counties—larger than both George Washington's Mount Vernon and Thomas Jefferson's Monticello combined. In 1899, Smithsonia had a workforce of over a thousand, including both "free" and forced laborers.

Poverty trapped many Black people in servitude to white landowners like Smith. "The white folks had all the courts, all the guns, all the hounds . . . all the money, and nearly all the land—and we had only our ignorance, our poverty and our empty hands," one man recalled.[27] Without property, income, or a fixed address, formerly enslaved individuals and their descendants had to work as sharecroppers to survive.

In the sharecropping system, landowners, typically former slaveholders, permitted laborers to cultivate their land in exchange for a portion of the crops produced. Workers signed contracts and took out loans from plantation stores, known as commissaries, to pay for supplies such as seeds, tools, and equipment, which were often overpriced. Unfortunately, if a crop failed, the workers became indebted to both the landowner and the shopkeeper. Many Black sharecroppers struggled to meet their crop quotas, resulting in a cycle of poverty that often led to incarceration and debt slavery.

If a worker signed a contract with a landowner and then left without paying their debts, they could be arrested and imprisoned. In such cases, sharecroppers were returned to their employers by the courts and forced to work until their debts were paid off—some never regained their freedom.

Occasionally, family members were able to purchase the freedom of their loved ones. Some arranged for their own labor to serve as payment for debts while others paid merchants to negotiate with plantation bosses for a family member's release. Yet these payments rarely covered the full amount owed. The price of freedom fluctuated, often surpassing the original amount of a person's debt.

Mentha Morrison could not afford to purchase freedom for her husband, Jackson. A judge had fined him one hundred dollars for a minor violation, a hefty sum for a low-income family like the Morrisons. The judge then sold his debt to a farmer, Moses Jordan, who later traded it to James Monroe Smith.

Jackson's debts kept growing with each transfer, leaving his wife no other choice but to pawn her labor to Smith to speed up the repayment process. For eighteen months, Mentha "worked like a man," enduring "all kinds of weather, rain, cold, and all." She even had to care for her nursing infant while toiling in the fields.[28]

Like most plantation bosses, Smith made no distinction between his free laborers, like Mentha, and his incarcerated workforce. He exploited them equally, whether they arrived in chains or bound to a contract. In the fields, Mentha worked shoulder to shoulder with debt slaves and slaves of the state. From daybreak to dusk, they plunged metal-tipped shovels into the soil, planting seeds and watering them with sweat leaked from their brows. At night, they washed their cracked, splintered palms with warm, salty tears and rested their overworked bodies on beds of wood and cotton. Boundless fields and humble shacks framed their suffering, ruled by Smith and his team of overseers.

Smith leased several women prisoners from the state of Georgia and assigned them to two of his plantations. Some were sent to Smithsonia, while others went to Oglethorpe, a smaller plantation. Among them were

Mary Martin and Mary Battle. While we are fortunate to know their names, many others remain unidentified.

In 1901, a Black woman whose name remains unknown was leased to Smith as a prisoner. Historical records provide no information about her age, her marital status, or whether she had children. It is also unclear how long she was forced to work and what her duties were, as there is no record of her occupation; she might have labored as a field hand, house servant, or cook—or even as a concubine. Smith was a bachelor.

With the details of her confinement missing from the historical record, one is left to wonder how this woman fared in Smith's custody. Was she forced to labor under the blazing sun and cold-blooded stares of overseers? Did she suffer beneath the weight of solid leather and white-hot rage that collided against her skin? Did she survive long enough to flee Smithsonia? Or, with bandages clinging to her back like bloody angel wings, did her soul finally fly home to freedom? We will never know.

At the height of the harvest season, Mentha found herself with an empty account. Despite working for eighteen months, she had earned very little, and Smith refused to acknowledge that Jackson's debt had been settled. Mentha was left with no other choice but to walk away. To avoid a lifetime of servitude, Jackson fled.

Before he could reunite with Mentha and their baby, Jackson was arrested and sent back to Smithsonia. Although the Thirteenth Amendment prohibited peonage, the criminal legal system upheld its practice by making it a crime to run away. White landowners like James Monroe Smith depended on legal officials such as magistrates to help recapture peons through criminal warrants. They also utilized the jail system to hold these individuals until they could reclaim them.

In the early 1900s, the US Department of Justice conducted an investigation of the Southern peonage system. This investigation provided Black women with a rare opportunity to report abusive labor practices to the federal government. However, it was not the first time Black women had testified before white officials. As early as 1866, survivors of the Memphis, Tennessee, massacre, like Lucy Smith, testified before a committee appointed by the US House of Representatives. In 1871, other survivors testified in congressional hearings on Ku Klux Klan violence, sharing stories similar to those of peonage survivors. Throughout American history, Black women have bravely used their voices to defend themselves and their families. Mentha Morrison exemplified this courage when she wrote a letter to President Theodore Roosevelt:

> Mr. President . . . I write to you this letter to inform you that my husband (Jackson, Morrison, col'd) is being made to serve an unlawful term at Col. James M. Smith's camp at Smithsonia, Ga., in Oglethorpe county . . . I appeal to you, as the Executive Head of our Nation to please do something for my husband. Will you please cause an investigation of that Camp to be made in the future, and while doing so it will be found that there are numbers of persons (both men and women) serving as slaves there for many months and days after their terms have expired.[29]

The outcome of the Morrisons' situation remains uncertain.

Mattie Youngblood's case provides a powerful example of a Black woman receiving justice in the end. In April 1901, Mattie was arrested for gambling and fined fifty dollars, along with seventy-five dollars in court fees. What began as a "small game of poker" turned out to be a costly mistake. But the agreement she made with Sheriff Simeon D. May to work as his cook ended up costing her much more.[30]

As the sheriff of Crenshaw County, Alabama, May had privileged access to misdemeanor prisoners, including Mattie. He could purchase their labor from the court and rearrest them if they tried to leave his custody. This was a unique power among those who exploited debt slaves, as they often relied on sheriffs for enforcement—and May was the sheriff.

Mattie worked her fingers to the bone, earning just one dollar a week. She believed her freedom depended on it. Little did she realize that by signing a contract with May, she had unintentionally sold herself into slavery.

After thirty months and four days of service, Mattie "abandoned her work." In other words, she quit. But May refused to let her go, using his power to arrest her for "violating a labor contract."[31]

Mattie was sentenced to "work out" new fines and costs totaling $27.85. What she did not know was that the governor had already remitted her original penalty—nearly *two years* before her second conviction. May tricked her into believing she was working off a debt, but he planned to keep her in slavery.

In February 1905, an Alabama federal grand jury indicted May on peonage charges. The warrant was "sworn out by Mat Youngblood" who, under oath, accused the sheriff of this crime. It was an unusual victory; rarely, if ever, was a white man indicted on the word of a Black woman. Justice was served for Mattie, but for countless others, their testimonies were never heard or were swiftly dismissed.

The US government formally abolished peonage in the 1940s. However, it is crucial to acknowledge that the practice never ended in places like Mississippi, where an undocumented number of Black women, men, and children still live and work on large plantations, earning less than eight dollars a day. On these twenty-first century peonage farms, "you don't see a lot of field hands in the fields picking crops like you would have during the period of sharecropping or chattel slavery," Antoinette Harrell explains. "Now you see machines, and you see people working around the equipment . . . you see the women who will cook the food and bring it to the Big House."[32]

From a jail cell in Macon, Georgia, in May 1915, a Black woman cook gave an order. She told the sergeant to call her employer, "a well known doctor," and "tell him if he wanted to eat breakfast . . . he had better come down and have the family cook released." She further warned, "If anybody misses a doctor from church this morning it's because he hasn't gotten that cook out of the police barracks in time to get the Sunday meal ready."[33]

At the time of the woman's arrest, Macon faced a shortage of Black cooks. The "cook problem" affected two-thirds of the city's white housewives, who were most frustrated by the lack of labor. Black women were equally dissatisfied with their poor treatment and low wages. Many decided they would no longer work, "as long as they could get a loaf of bread for five cents, and a glass of beer."[34] Their resistance had consequences; being labeled a "vagrant" resulted in imprisonment for some.

In the decades following the Civil War, Black domestic workers faced a high risk of incarceration. They were often fined and jailed over false accusations of theft or "disorderly conduct." Additionally, if they decided to quit their jobs, their white employers could have them taken into custody.

When three thousand Black washerwomen went on strike in Atlanta in 1881, city authorities mobilized to have them arrested. They were punished for what amounted to "stealing their labor," a "crime" comparable to property theft. Among those arrested was Sarah A. Collier, who received a twenty-dollar fine and a forty-day sentence on the chain gang.[35]

The exploitation of Black women on chain gangs became increasingly common after 1865. Through this method of punishment, counties forced individuals convicted of misdemeanors to engage in unpaid labor. Even simple acts of survival, such as stealing food, could result in fines or imprisonment on a chain gang for up to a year.

It was a warm day in March 1891 when the police vehicle nicknamed the "Black Maria of Bibb County," made its usual stop at City Hall. The "chain gang driver," who had done this many times before, waited patiently as the sergeant called out the names of the prisoners for the day's "load." Among them were three men and one woman, one of at least 2,680 Black women sentenced to the Georgia chain gang.[36]

How this woman ended up on the sergeant's docket remains unclear. One is left to wonder whether she was a victim of Macon's poverty or a casualty of its "cook problem." What is clear, however, is that the punishment she received—being forced to labor on a chain gang—was worse than any crime she could have possibly committed.

The cruel punishment of Black women for minor "crimes" is well-documented. Historical records reveal that Black women were frequently arrested for trivial offenses such as "running dirty water in the streets," "operating a wagon without a badge [permit]," and "blocking the sidewalk." Arrests were also common for quality-of-life misdemeanors like theft, vagrancy, prostitution, selling bootleg liquor, public drinking, loitering, fighting, using offensive language, disturbing the peace, and disorderly conduct. When individuals could not pay the fines imposed on them, judges would sentence them to jail or hard labor on a county chain gang.[37]

Lizzie Boatright and her family faced difficulty paying the fifty dollars in fines and costs that would have kept her from being sent to the chain gang. In March 1897, a judge convicted the eighteen-year-old of stealing clothing worth approximately five dollars. As they were living below the poverty line, Lizzie and her relatives lacked the resources to buy her freedom. Therefore, she was forced to serve six months on a Georgia chain gang.

Two months into Lizzie's sentence, a special inspector appointed by the governor found her working as a man. "I called her out from among the gang and away from the guard," said the inspector. He barely noticed her womanhood hidden beneath her baggy striped uniform. At the sound of his voice, Lizzie dropped her "short-handled spade" and followed him to a private area, where he questioned her about the guard, Bob Cannon. She confided in him about her abuse: "Mr. Cannon made me take down my britches and lean over and then he whipped me."[38]

The inspector appealed to Governor William Atkinson to remove Lizzie from the camp. "It is too bad for even the worst of male criminals, and no woman should be permitted to remain in it for a moment," he wrote. It was an unusual plea for mercy; rarely were Black women regarded as "women" or deemed worthy of protection by white men. But in Lizzie's case, the governor granted her clemency and allowed her to return home.

Lizzie Boatright was one of the thousands of Black women sentenced to work in road gangs. These construction crews lined every Southern highway, marching shackled together in a formation that resembled a slave chain gang or coffle. Each day, they traveled from one worksite to another, sometimes riding in cages and at other times walking. The clanking of their chains could be heard for miles.

Dora Freeman ate, slept, and worked in leg irons, just like the men beside her. The bonds were placed on her after a judge sentenced her to a Georgia chain gang for theft, turning a trivial offense into twelve months of backbreaking labor. Although the exact kind of work she did is unclear, she may have performed roadbuilding tasks such as breaking rocks, shoveling dirt, and hauling heavy loads of clay.

Dora's days in the road camp were long and hard, and nighttime offered no rest. Days into her confinement, a man "connected with the chain gang" sexually assaulted her, turning a routine transfer into a night of terror. When asked about her whereabouts, a guard admitted she had disappeared. "Four women were to be transferred from the camp . . . but the men who took them left two behind," he confirmed.[39]

During the period when Dora was being raped, her husband fought to have her released from the road gang. He scrimped and saved as much money as possible—freedom fees were not cheap. After one month, he had raised enough to pay her fine. Dora's spouse prevailed in this unusual love story, proving his devotion to her was stronger than the chains holding her.

Dora experienced incarceration in the state that held the most Black women on chain gangs. However, it is crucial to acknowledge that other states also exploited Black women's labor through this system. In Texas, for instance, Black women were sentenced to work on county road gangs. In South Carolina, they served time working in county rock piles or on the streets, sweeping and collecting garbage alongside male prisoners.

Similarly, in Kansas, women who could not pay their fines were forced to "don bloomers and take their place on the 'chain gang'" with men.[40]

Historically, most chain gangs in America were composed of Black men. However, some states had all-Black female work crews. In 1897, a chain gang known as the Calico Chain Gang was established in Jackson, Mississippi. The group consisted of twelve Black women—Sylvella Palmer, Amanda Johnston, Minnie Johnston, Susie Wills, Ida Lewis, Mary Bullock, Ida Williams, Belle Oliver, Emma Hillard, Goldie Fleming, Sarah Jackson, and Annie Starks—who had all been convicted of vagrancy and sentenced to clean the city's streets. Only eight women ultimately served on the gang, as four managed to pay their fines.[41]

The sight of an all-Black female chain gang left city residents speechless. They had never seen Black women "serving time on the streets" or police officers supervising their work. The exploitation of Black women typically occurred in private spaces, not on public thoroughfares, but white Mississippi authorities changed that, using the chain gang to publicly reinforce Black women's oppression and warn them of the consequences of poverty. Their hostility could be summed up in one sentence: "[T]he way they sling the hoe and rake is a caution to other lazy, worthless negro women who infest the city and make their living otherwise than by the sweat of their brow."[42]

Nearly a century after Mississippi's Calico Chain Gang, Sheriff Joe Arpaio established a similar chain gang in Maricopa County, Arizona. In 1995, he recruited a group of primarily undocumented Latina women to pull weeds and bury unclaimed bodies in exchange for time out of their cells. In essence, he offered them hard time or hard labor. It was an unfair trade, but a last resort for those who wanted to escape twenty-three-hour lockdowns in Estrella Jail.

"I'll do anything to get out of jail," said Ernestine White. She negotiated the terms of her freedom, exchanging iron bars for leg irons and an orange jumpsuit with the words "Sheriff's Chain Gang" stamped across the back. Although she did not descend from enslaved Black ancestors, she knew how it felt to be labeled as property and to have her oppression made public; the sheriff insisted that she and other women work in plain sight. "I don't want them out in the desert chopping rocks," he demanded. "I want them out in the open where everybody can see them and show people that this could happen to them if they commit a crime."[43]

Although America's self-proclaimed toughest sheriff credited himself with being the first to put women in leg irons, history proves this claim to be false. Still, Arpaio's establishment of an all-female chain gang in Arizona offers important lessons about slavery's legacies: the consequences of slavery now extend to other racial and ethnic groups, and women of various races and ethnicities can suffer under a system originally designed to control and punish Black women.

Across America today, Black women are still locked in chains. Many lose their freedom for minor infractions—what some call "broken windows crimes"—such as driving with a broken taillight, failing to pay a parking ticket, and jaywalking while Black. Those unable to pay fines, fees, or bail remain trapped in a form of debt slavery.

It is a fact that Black women are three times more likely than white women to be arrested, fined, and jailed.[44] The US Department of Justice documented some of these racial disparities following the 2015 killing of Michael Brown. After Darren Wilson, a white Ferguson, Missouri, police officer, shot and killed the unarmed teenager, the Justice Department launched an investigation that resulted in the landmark Ferguson Report.

This report revealed how Ferguson's law enforcement system, including its courts, exercised unlawful bias against Black residents. Despite making up 67 percent of the population, "African Americans accounted for 85 percent of FPD's traffic stops, 90 percent of FPD's citations, and 93 percent of FPD's arrests from 2012 to 2014."[45] Investigators concluded that Ferguson's law enforcement practices were "shaped by the City's focus on revenue rather than by public safety needs."[46]

After illegally parking her car in Ferguson, a Black woman was fined $1,000 and spent six nights in jail; her original fine was $151. At the time of her arrest in 2007, she experienced severe financial hardship and homelessness. Despite her circumstances, the court charged her with seven failure to appear offenses for missing court dates and failing to pay her parking tickets. Each failure to appear charge resulted in another arrest warrant and more fines and fees. When she tried to make partial payments toward her debts, the court returned them, "refusing to accept anything less than payment in full."[47]

Historically, the criminal legal system has demonstrated a persistent bias against Black women, subjecting them to exorbitant fees for their freedom. This is exemplified in cases like the one in Ferguson and numerous others from the past. For instance, in April 1931, Flora Jones Moore was arrested for forging $13.50 in checks to pay for groceries at a New Orleans store. Her bail was set at an outrageous $2,500. In 2016, Twanda Marshinda Brown was fined $2,300 for two parking tickets. When she fell behind on payments, she was sent to jail in Lexington County, South Carolina, for fifty-seven days. The consequences of her incarceration for poverty were tragic. "I cried every day," she remembered. "I lost my new job and the chance to get a promotion and a raise. I spent my fortieth birthday in jail. But even worse was the fear that my thirteen-year-old son would be taken away from me by the Department of Social Services."[48]

Even with recent bail reform initiatives, women like Twanda are still waiting for trial dates or remain in jail as "debtors." Cash bail remains a pervasive issue in the United States, with forty-two states still requiring it, despite its negative impacts that date back one hundred years ago, when Belle Griffin and Clara Anderson faced similar conditions. Reflecting on the ongoing dangers of cash bail and debt slavery in Galveston, Texas, former American Civil Liberties Union senior staff attorney Twyla Carter issues a powerful warning: "If you are accused of a crime and arrested . . . you better hope you can afford to pay the preset bail amount to get out of jail. If not, then you will join hundreds of other people who are incarcerated simply because they cannot afford to buy their freedom."[49]

The criminalization of poor Black women spans generations, as does debt slavery. Although Black women are no longer bought and sold at auctions, courts continue to monetize their freedom and confine them through unnecessary arrests and predatory revenue tactics. In America today, jails remain a powerful tool of oppression, similar to what existed during the height of the domestic slave trade and the post-Emancipation prisoner trade. Prisons have also exploited Black women, from forcing them to rebuild the South after the Civil War to requiring them to sew masks during the COVID-19 pandemic. For over 150 years, the US prison system has profited from their labor and punishment—a history often overlooked, yet central to the next chapter of this story.

Delia Garlic, survivor of the domestic slave trade, c. 1936.

Enslaved woman incarcerated at a slave jail in Alexandria, Virginia, c. 1861.

VIEW OF THE INTERIOR OF THE JAIL IN WASHINGTON.—FANNY JACKSON.

Fanny Jackson and her children at the Washington, DC, jail, 1836.

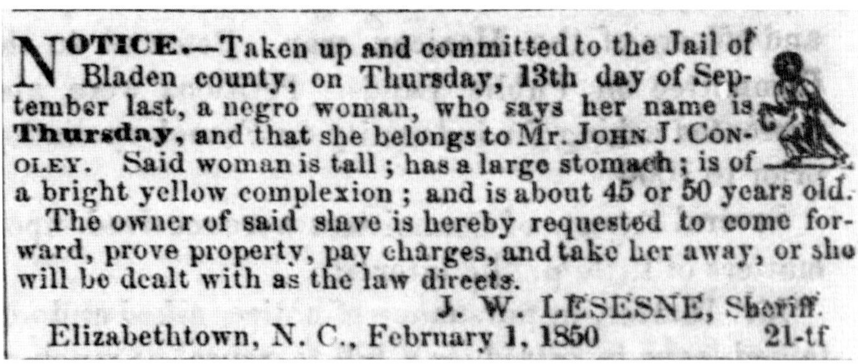

NOTICE.—Taken up and committed to the Jail of Bladen county, on Thursday, 13th day of September last, a negro woman, who says her name is **Thursday**, and that she belongs to Mr. John J. Conoley. Said woman is tall; has a large stomach; is of a bright yellow complexion; and is about 45 or 50 years old.

The owner of said slave is hereby requested to come forward, prove property, pay charges, and take her away, or she will be dealt with as the law directs.

J. W. LESESNE, Sheriff.

Elizabethtown, N. C., February 1, 1850 21-tf

Jail commitment notification for capture of Thursday, a woman incarcerated for escaping enslavement.

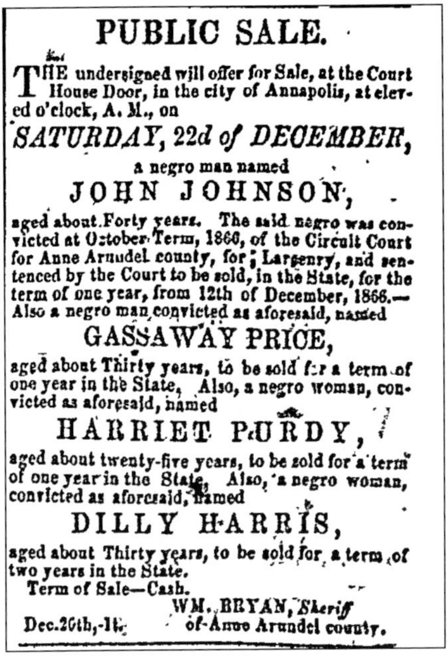

PUBLIC SALE.

THE undersigned will offer for Sale, at the Court House Door, in the city of Annapolis, at eleven o'clock, A. M., on

SATURDAY, 22d of DECEMBER,

a negro man named

JOHN JOHNSON,

aged about Forty years. The said negro was convicted at October Term, 1866, of the Circuit Court for Anne Arundel county, for Larceny, and sentenced by the Court to be sold, in the State, for the term of one year, from 12th of December, 1866.—Also a negro man convicted as aforesaid, named

GASSAWAY PRICE,

aged about Thirty years, to be sold for a term of one year in the State. Also, a negro woman, convicted as aforesaid, named

HARRIET PURDY,

aged about twenty-five years, to be sold for a term of one year in the State. Also, a negro woman, convicted as aforesaid, named

DILLY HARRIS,

aged about Thirty years, to be sold for a term of two years in the State.

Term of Sale—Cash.

WM. BRYAN, *Sheriff* of Anne Arundel county.

Dec. 20th,-1[illegible]

(LEFT) Advertisement for the sale of Harriet Purdy, 1866.

(BOTTOM) Mary Morst pregnant with twins, Virginia State Penitentiary, 1912.

Women prisoners on Juneteenth at Goree State Prison Farm for Women, Huntsville, Texas, June 19, 1919.

Mary Prince on White House grounds with Amy Carter.

CHAPTER 4

PROFITING PRISONS

Nora waited patiently for the Gwaltney family to leave for their Sunday night church service before going to their house. Only months earlier, Mrs. Gwaltney had welcomed Nora into the family's home as a servant. She assigned daily tasks, which included cooking dinner for the family on a wood-burning stove, using logs that Nora might have chopped herself, and setting the dining room table with carefully polished silverware and fine china, which she gently cleaned after scrubbing their dirty laundry. However, this evening was different. Nora had not come to the Gwaltney home to work. She had returned to burn it down.

Nora never explained her reasons for setting fire to the house. Perhaps being dismissed pushed her over the edge; just before destroying her workplace, she had been fired. Other motives may have driven her to seek revenge, such as an unpaid debt or a deep-seated resentment toward Mrs. Gwaltney. It was alleged that Nora took her clothing and jewelry before turning her bedroom into a pile of ashes.

Nora's plans to dress like Mrs. Gwaltney ultimately failed. Black-and-white stripes, coarse leather brogans, and chains—the uniform for every prisoner, including women, in the state of Georgia—became her new wardrobe. But Nora had not yet legally become a woman. At the time of her conviction, she was only seventeen years old.

In April 1891, Nora was sentenced to ninety-nine years in prison—the longest determinate sentence ever inflicted on a person in the state of Georgia.[1] The punishment was extreme, even for a Black woman. While not uncommon, Nora's sentence revealed firsthand the racial inequities in Georgia's judicial system. It also exposed the racial disparities in punishment that plagued Black women throughout the United States—racism was never only a Southern issue.

The same day an all-white jury found Nora Lay guilty of arson, Ora McKee, a white woman, was acquitted of murder despite evidence of her guilt. Notably, both trials occurred in the same courtroom in Rome, Georgia, presided over by the same judge. However, their outcomes—and the experiences of most Black and white women in the judicial system—were strikingly different.

Ora had access to a legal team of white men to defend her, while Nora chose to fight her own case. When asked if she wanted counsel, Nora boldly replied, "I represent myself."[2] Ora also had middle-class resources and the privilege of white womanhood to shield her from the consequences of her alleged crime. In contrast, Nora had poverty and Black skin, which hindered her ability to be found innocent or shown mercy in any court of law.

The state decided not to execute Nora. Instead, it stripped away everything that could have given her life meaning. This included the chance to grow old with her husband, to raise strong children, to pursue an education, to earn wages, to own property, and to build wealth within her community—a wild dream, but one that freed people held onto even when they knew their circumstances would not permit it. It also stripped her of her constitutional rights to freedom and citizenship.

Being labeled a felon condemned Nora to a life in chains. Having never experienced enslavement, she did not yet know what it meant to be treated as a captive or human commodity, or to have her worth measured by the value of her labor. But all of that would soon change.

Following her sentencing, Nora became the official property of the state of Georgia. She was leased to James Warren English, the owner of the notorious Chattahoochee Brick Company in Atlanta and forced to remain in his possession for a year and a half. However, after giving prison life "a few weeks' trial, and, finding that it did not suit," Nora made her escape.[3]

"Twenty-five dollars reward is offered for her capture," reported the *Atlanta Constitution* newspaper about Nora. The announcement read like a fugitive slave advertisement, complete with a detailed physical description: "height, five feet, one inch; weight, 123 pounds; color, very light mulatto; long black hair, keen black eyes, chunky and heavy set." And it served a similar purpose—to publicly reinforce Nora's status as a "criminal."[4]

Nora violated the law by stealing her liberty. She committed a common "offense" among captive people. But her greater "crime" was denying the state of Georgia and its private contractor future earnings from her forced labor. Nora ran quickly and desperately, yet she could not outpace the dogs, armed posse, and white press summoned to hunt her down. Eventually, they caught up with her and returned her to captivity. Still, Nora kept running. Less than a month after being captured, Nora ran away again. She fled prison a total of four times, scaling a fourteen-foot fence, jumping from a moving train, wading through a river, and building a temporary home in the woods. Caught by Captain Starnes, an authority in the prison system, after her first escape, she explained her reason for wanting to return to Rome, Georgia: "For the purpose of killing the woman who told on me, so that I could hang."[5]

Millions of Black women in America have walked in Nora's shoes. They have endured Jane Crow's injustices and weathered its carceral consequence: enslavement. The ratification of the Thirteenth Amendment brought dramatic changes to the lives of Black individuals. They gained the right to universal freedom for the first time in American history. Yet they also became more vulnerable to re-enslavement through the prison system.

Covering more than 150 years, this chapter traces the evolution of America's prison system from the aftermath of the Civil War to the War on Drugs. It examines how the rise of freedom gave way to profit-driven systems of state-sponsored mass incarceration designed to perpetuate slavery: convict leasing, state-run prison farms, and both public and private for-profit prisons. Furthermore, it reveals the little-known story of Black women whose forced labor helped build America into the profitable "prison nation" it is today.

Sister Rose Henderson felt the Spirit during her regular Sunday school service at the Bolton broom factory, owned by prison contractor James W. English. She began "patting her dainty brogans on the floor and clapping her hands while she hummed a low tune." Then, suddenly, with a fervent shout she exclaimed: "Oh, bless God! bless Jesus! I'se done save, I'se going home."[6]

The promise of Heaven excited Rose. As an incarcerated person, she could not count on the promises of the Thirteenth Amendment to set her free. And while she prayed for the state of Georgia to grant her clemency, she knew better than to put her hope in white men or their systems. She put her faith in God instead.

From birth, Rose was denied her human right to freedom. She came into the world as an enslaved person, born to parents who had survived the domestic slave trade. They traveled from Virginia in chains, passing through at least one private slave jail on their way to the Georgia auction block. Somewhere along the way, either during or after their journey, they welcomed Rose, in 1844.

When Rose began her life as a legally free person in 1865, she was only twenty-one. She had her whole life ahead of her, even if the aftermath of freedom made survival uncertain. Perhaps she dared to envision a life in freedom anyway—a stable family, a piece of land, and a legal marriage—all the things that her parents had been denied under chattel slavery. What she did not anticipate was a lifetime of re-enslavement.

In 1877, Rose's dreams came to a startling end when she was convicted of murder and sentenced to life in prison. Her conviction coincided with the end of Reconstruction in the South, ushering in a new era of inequality. As the state of Georgia prepared to lease Rose to a private company, the US government was withdrawing its support for the formerly enslaved. The declining commitment to protect Black freedom rights and citizenship came as control of the South shifted to white Southerners, who employed violence and legal measures to suppress Black social, economic, and political progress (for men) and entrench racial inequality.

Even without her imprisonment, Rose would have felt the impact of this inequality in daily life. State laws enforcing segregation would have prevented her from sitting in the "whites-only" section on public transportation and in theaters, restaurants, and other public spaces. If she had received an education, she would have been forced to attend all-Black schools, whether she wanted to or not. She would have also been forced to witness the increased violence that plagued her community after the federal troops left the South, even though their protection of Black lives had never been fully effective.

Regardless of being incarcerated, Rose still endured the injustices of Jane Crow, though in ways not commonly associated with post-Reconstruction racial discrimination. During her court trial, for example, Jane Crow showed up in the form of an all-white jury, despite Rose's constitutional right to stand before a jury of her peers. After her conviction, it appeared in the racially biased prison system that confined her, and countless other Black women, while white women entered the system in only single-digit numbers. And following her sentencing, it emerged again as a train car, or horse-drawn wagon, used to transport her into the hands of a private investor eager to profit from her labor.

In freedom's aftermath, prisons served one main purpose: profit. This was especially true in the Southern region, which, after 1865, continued to be the epicenter of mass incarceration. Unlike mass jailing, profit-driven prison systems held fewer people but for longer durations, not because of the severity of their alleged crimes but because long sentences served the interests of businesses. Prisons became the primary labor providers for investors seeking a cheap, dependable workforce.[7]

The end of chattel slavery marked a shift from private ownership to public control of Black people's bodies. In the former slave states, the prison system took on the role of enslaver. To generate profits, it formed partnerships with private companies and individuals through a practice known as convict leasing.

Convict leasing was essentially a public system of slave hiring, except the slaves in this system were prisoners. Under this system, state governments solicited bids from companies and individuals seeking to hire prison labor. However, the process was selective: most states limited their business to notable white men, including wealthy entrepreneurs, senators, governors, ex-slaveholders, former slave traders, and Klansmen. Investors with the most competitive offers would be permitted to lease state prisoners for a fee.

Like slave hiring, convict leasing was a racially specific practice. Though sometimes compared to the the early nineteenth-century contract labor system, when white men made up most of the US prison population, the two systems were not the same. As unusual as it may seem, white men were protected by institutions where they endured punishment; before 1865, they left prison only to fight for the Confederacy in exchange for pardons.[8] It was not until after the Civil War—when convict leasing was introduced—that states began hiring out prison labor beyond the walls.

After Emancipation, the exploitation of prison labor for profit became increasingly tied to race. Although the practice of incarcerating individuals based on race had roots in chattel slavery, it did not extend to the prison system at first. The introduction of convict leasing fundamentally transformed American punishment by creating the nation's first racially driven, for-profit prison systems.

Almost overnight, institutions that had primarily incarcerated white men suddenly became overwhelmingly Black. Racism dramatically altered the demographics of Southern prisons: by 1870 over 90 percent of prisoners were Black men, and 90 percent of female prisoners were Black women.

The convict lease system contributed significantly to this trend, as did the individuals hiring prison labor. Their emerging businesses fueled the demand for punishment, creating an additional incentive for mass incarceration. As Southern industries grew, Black prison rates surged.

States turned to private companies to detain the increasing prison population. By collaborating with private industry, they effectively committed to supplying labor for railroads, mines, factories, farms, lumber mills, and even universities being developed throughout the South. In exchange, lessees agreed to make payments to the state and to provide shelter, food, clothing, and medical care, as well as to administer punishments and burials for those who died in their custody.

Although state governments were the primary architects of the convict leasing system, they did not act alone. Without white judges and juries to ensure racially biased convictions, there would have been no labor force to lease. And without state legislatures approving partnerships between states and private companies, the convict leasing system would have never existed.

Convict leasing formalized the relationship between the private sector and state governments, ensuring wealth for generations of white men and women who profited from it. Through this system, former slaveholders, who had lost their fortunes due to the war, found new ways to achieve prosperity, ultimately becoming some of the nation's wealthiest landowners. White businessmen who had never owned enslaved individuals or financially benefited from enslavement gained control over hundreds of people, sometimes even more than a thousand.

Over the sixty-year duration of convict leasing, lessees accumulated great wealth, amassing fortunes that rivaled those of slave traders and enslavers. By today's economic standards, most were millionaires. But some counted earnings in the billions.

The world's first billion-dollar company, United States Steel Corporation (U.S. Steel), gained part of its wealth from leasing incarcerated people in its Alabama mines. Founded by Andrew Carnegie, J. P. Morgan, and Charles Schwab, this company emerged to become the world's largest steel producer and corporation. At its peak, in the early 1900s, it was valued at $1.4 billion, or approximately $53 billion today. It is one of the best documented historical examples of a major American corporation profiting from prison labor, a practice that grew more popular during the War on Drugs.[9]

In addition to U.S. Steel, numerous other companies profited from convict leasing. The Texas-based Imperial Sugar Company contracted prisoners to work in its sugarcane fields. The Tennessee Coal and Iron Company employed prison labor in its coal mines. The Putnam Lumber Company in Florida utilized prisoners in its lumber factories. The Georgia-based Chattahoochee Brick Company used prison labor to produce bricks and brooms. The Pratt Coal & Coke Company used Alabama prisoners to mine high-grade ore. Even Clemson University in South Carolina employed prison labor to construct its buildings.

These companies represent only a fraction of the businesses that exploited prison labor—and Black women. Countless others, including private landowners, also invested in this practice. While most private landowners depended on debt slavery for labor, some utilized the prison system as well.

Overall, private companies and private individuals profited the most from convict leasing. However, states also profited significantly from this practice. By 1898, 73 percent of Alabama's revenue came from leasing prisoners—nearly $100,000 annually. These figures increased substantially during the early twentieth century, with the state earning over $2 million from prison labor between 1910 and 1914.[10] By the time the system ended in 1928, Alabama had generated more profit from convict leasing than any other state in America.

Like Alabama, Georgia also generated substantial profits from convict leasing. In response to the high demand for prison labor, the Georgia legislature passed a law in 1876 allowing companies to pay $25,000 annually for a twenty-year lease. This lengthy contract highlighted the system's economic importance to the state. It effectively guaranteed long-term assets from a prison population it pledged to expand.

Rose Henderson entered Georgia's convict lease system just as the twenty-year lease began. At this time, the contracting firm Grant, Alexander, and Company secured hundreds of prisoners to build the Georgia Air-Line Railroad, including Rose.[11] Having survived chattel slavery, she knew about hard labor. But nothing could have prepared her for the grueling demands of railroad construction.

Rose spent the first thirteen years of her life sentence grinding on the rails. Though her exact responsibilities are unknown, she may have labored in the "cuts" (railroad excavation sites), leveling the ground, moving drift to the "fills" (large rock heaps), or shoveling dirt. Grant, Alexander, and Company assigned most of its female labor force to this detail. Yet it is possible that Rose performed duties reserved for the state's strongest men. Maybe she cut the trees to make the railroad ties or assisted with installing the massive iron rails. None of these possibilities are farfetched given the undifferentiating exploitation of Black women's labor in Georgia's convict leasing system. In the Empire State, women prisoners did the same jobs as men, and lessees paid the same amount for their labor.

Georgia's unique reliance on Black women's labor sets it apart from other convict leasing states, along with its having the most industries after 1865. Widely known for being the industrial leader of the "New South"—a term used to describe the region's focus on modernizing and industrializing after the Civil War—Georgia also served as the convict leasing capital of America. This was due to its extensive industries and large number of lessees: fourteen in 1876. It also stemmed from the state's sophisticated business model. More than a hundred years before private prison stocks became popular in the 1990s, investors could buy shares in its public prison system. In fact, owning shares in one of Georgia's incorporated prison companies was required to bid on incarcerated labor.

Because of its vast partnerships, Georgia divided its system into three prison companies. The largest of these companies was Penitentiary Company No. 3. Beginning in the 1880s, it came to dominate the state's prison labor market, with James W. English at the helm. By the late 1890s, English controlled the majority of Georgia's incarcerated labor force, making him the state's largest hirer of prison labor.

In 1897 alone, English controlled 1,206 of Georgia's 2,235 prisoners, more than any other lessee in the state. He worked most of them at his Atlanta brick factory, the headquarters for the Chattahoochee Brick Company, established in 1878. With his extensive labor force, English built one of the nation's largest brick companies, producing an average of 30 million bricks per year. At its peak, his company generated more than $200,000 annually—roughly $7 million today.[12]

Mattie Crawford, Mollie White, Nora Daniel, Ella Gamble, Emma Clark, Eliza Randall, Minnie Ward, Leila Burgess, Kate Clark, and Susan Hill were among the women who played a role in building James English's brick empire. At his Atlanta factory, these women mined clay and molded bricks. They also endured severe beatings for resisting their bondage.

Although English had never been an enslaver, and "Captain" James T. Casey, the man he hired to serve as his "whipping boss," had never been an overseer, both excelled in their roles. Their backgrounds were nearly as humble as those of the women and men they abused: English was a former orphan, and Casey was the son of a ferryman and a homemaker. Yet both gained success, creating new family legacies built on punishment for profit.

As a whipping boss, Casey acquired two skills that his parents never had: reading and writing. He honed those skills at the Chattahoochee Brick Company, keeping an extensive record of the violence he inflicted on Black women and the acts of resistance they courageously displayed. "Leila Burgess," "13 licks," "talking back"; "Nora Daniel," "10 strokes," "fighting"; "Kate Clarke," "25 licks," "fighting"; and "Susan Hill," "25 licks," "fighting" are among the many entries in the "whipping reports"

Casey kept for the company and the state of Georgia. These ledgers are some of the only existing evidence of Black women's lives at the Chattahoochee Brick Factory; they have proven essential to the study of Black women and convict leasing.[13]

In the spring of 1890, James English shifted into a new enterprise: broom making. He envisioned using his all-female labor force to make enough brooms to "sweep the state of Georgia." However, instead of stitching brooms, the women focused on building a community.

After a thirteen-year stint on the Air-Line Railroad, Rose was moved to the Bolton broom factory, where she joined Nora Lay, Ella Gamble, Lila Echols, Psyche Hudson, and many other women from various convict lease camps. There, Rose established bonds of faith and sisterhood, allowing her to transform Camp Bolton from a place of punishment into a house of prayer. It is in this space where her soul ran free, even though she could not. And it is where Sister Clara Haynes found rest in God, despite her forced labor, declaring, "I'se tired on the way, but I find Jesus every day."[14]

Each time a new lessee claimed their labor, the women grew more tired. Those with life sentences, like Rose and Clara, had endured multiple forced migrations through the state's prison camps. They moved from one hirer to another, their experiences mirroring the domestic slave trade. By the time she arrived at Camp Heardmont prison plantation in 1892, Rose had spent nearly as many years enslaved by the state as she had under chattel slavery.

William Henry Mattox fought valiantly for the Confederacy, risking his life to defend the institution of slavery and the profits derived from the seventy-eight enslaved people he owned with his wife, Rebecca. When the war ended, they lost ownership of all of them but managed to retain their "Big House," land, and earnings. Mattox used the remaining income from his slaveholding business to create new opportunities within the Georgia state prison system.[15]

In 1892, Mattox secured a contract with the government of Georgia, agreeing to pay $12.50 per head, to lease sixty-four Black women from its prison system. He was granted unlimited access to their labor, while the state retained ownership of their bodies. Eager to secure a permanent facility for the state's female prisoners, officials hired out the entire female prison population to Mattox to work on his six-thousand-acre plantation, known as Camp Heardmont.[16]

Nora was only in the second year of her ninety-nine-year sentence when she arrived at Camp Heardmont. For the second time, she would be forced to carry the economic aspirations of a private investor on her back. The weight was immense. However, she did not have to bear it alone—Rose Henderson, Clara Haynes, and others were there to support her.

Life on Mattox's plantation was hard for all the women, including Nora. Even at her young age, she found it challenging to meet the demands of forced labor. Yet bearing witness to women like Rose, whose bodies had already been worn down by chattel slavery, who disappeared into the woods every morning to chop down trees for Mattox's cordwood business made it all the more unbearable.

Nora greeted women early in the morning as they arose from their beds never knowing if they would survive the day's work. Some succumbed to illness and extreme heat, while others fell victim to gunshot wounds inflicted by Mattox's guards. Though Nora may not have witnessed every death, she was likely present for at least one: while working in the fields one day, a woman collapsed and died from sunstroke. Nora was there, too, somewhere between the hoeing and plow gang.[17]

The shadow of death loomed over Nora during her many assignments at Camp Heardmont. It even followed her to the river, where she worked pulling flatboats transporting goods to and from the plantation. There, she waded through troubled waters—waters that bore witness to unimaginable cruelties.

The Broad River, once a hub of commercial activity, had become a floating graveyard for the youngest victims of convict leasing: Black infants. It is where innocent souls were rocked to sleep by rushing water.

It is where Black women's dreams of motherhood died before they had a chance to be fulfilled.

Sexual violence was a constant reality for Black women confined at Camp Heardmont. The abuse they endured reflected conditions in the outside world, where they lived under the continuous threat of being raped. Within the private world of the prison plantation, their circumstances were even more dire. Guards, whipping bosses, physicians, and lessees had unrestricted access to their bodies. Protected by the immunity granted to white men for crimes against Black women, they perpetuated a cycle of sexual violence and reproductive harm rooted in slavery.

So, what became of Black children born from the violence of white men? While chattel slavery allowed a white man to financially benefit from sexually abusing a Black woman, this was no longer the case after 1865. As Black women's reproductive capacities shifted from producing chattel to birthing citizens, there was no value attached to their wombs. Thus, children born to incarcerated mothers were deemed "disposable," as former enslavers no longer relied on them to increase their wealth, instead utilizing the prison system.

In his role as a lessee, Mattox viewed Black women merely as laborers, not as sources of life. His focus was on acquiring profits from them, not additional children who might reduce his earnings. To ensure Black women's full participation in the labor force, Mattox took extreme measures—even condoning murder. In fact, he commanded that any baby born on his plantation be buried in the river, the same river where Nora stood waiting for the boats.[18]

"To be candid with you I would not give those two hours and a half . . . if I did not want the mules to have the rest," William Henry Mattox told prominent Atlanta journalist Frank Weldon Johnson on a visit to Camp Heardmont. Caroline Crittenden appreciated the daily break from plowing, even if it arose from Mattox's desire to protect his animals. "I'm fifty-eight years old and been plowing in the fields all my life," she told

Johnson.[19] Crittenden struggled to get around as fast as the younger women but still possessed the skills to perform the job. Most of the others did not.

At Camp Heardmont, women were often assigned jobs for which they had no experience. This situation impacted almost all women in prison, regardless of where they were confined. The exploitative nature of prison labor meant that women were required to perform any tasks demanded of them, without consideration of their work experience.

Mattox turned cooks into field hands, laundresses into lumberjacks, and house servants into blacksmiths. He took advantage of the state's practice of forcing Black women prisoners into traditionally male labor jobs; in Georgia, "women's work" was an exception rather than the norm. Nevertheless, domestics and laundresses did not have it easy. Working in the "Big House" under Rebecca Allen Mattox, the mistress of Camp Heardmont, could be harder than working in the fields.

"Negroes are everywhere," noted Frank Weldon Johnson during his visit to the Mattox family home. "They are so numerous that they almost run over one another. They really do run." Mollie Pierce worked running rows in the cotton fields for almost a year before being "brought up from the quarters" to run in the Mattox family home. It was her first time working as a domestic servant while imprisoned. Before Mattox, the state had hired her out to James Monroe Smith, and she tilled the fields of Smithsonia for several years.[20]

As the Mattox family cook, Mollie encountered new difficulties and demands. If living in the quarters with other women had provided her a sense of community, working in the isolation of Rebecca Mattox's kitchen would have been a drastic change for her. The role exposed her to common challenges faced by Black women working in white women's households: constant supervision and scrutiny, unlimited demands on their time and energy, physical and verbal abuse, and condescension disguised as praise.

"The favorite among the lessee and his family is Molly." "Molly is not regarded as a convict and is not treated as one." "She seldom goes around the quarters."[21] Mollie's captors created lasting impressions on their invited guest, reinforcing the popular "good master, faithful slave" stereotype. Hidden in their descriptions of her loyalty and privileged status in their family was the truth: Mollie was not only the cook but had also been promoted to the role of "mammy."[22]

"The family will hate to give her up," the Mattox family shared with Johnson. They regretted the fact that her fifteen-year sentence would be ending soon, marking the expiration of her forced labor. But Mollie looked forward to leaving. She knew "exactly when she ought to get out, even to the day."[23]

The experiences of incarcerated domestics like Mollie remain underexplored in the history of convict leasing. However, an even less examined topic involves the role of white women. Who were these women, and what role did they play in exploiting prison labor? Some answers can be found in the story of Rebecca Mattox.

Rebecca Mattox's role in convict leasing provides a valuable perspective into the lives of women in this system. As the daughter of a slaveholding mother, a plantation mistress, and co-manager of a prison camp, Rebecca exemplifies how white women gained power by supporting state-sanctioned slavery and oppression of Black women. While the involvement of white women in convict leasing is an important part of our history, it has been largely overlooked.

Camp Heardmont prison plantation is named after Rebecca Mattox's grandfather, Stephen Heard. A prominent figure in Georgia, Heard was appointed the state's first governor in 1780. Before that, Heard was a war hero who fought in the French and Indian War under President George Washington and later in the American Revolution. For his military service in the American Revolution, Heard received a land grant of approximately six thousand acres, where he established the Heardmont slave plantation. Why a century later William Henry Mattox chose to name his prison plantation after the slave plantation founded by his wife's grandfather remains a mystery. He may have wanted to honor her family's legacy, including their connections to slaveholding.

Rebecca spent much of her youth watching her mother manage a large plantation. From the age of twelve, she observed her mother supervising the family's enslaved labor force, plantation staff, finances, and other business activities related to the estate. Depending on the type of enslaver her mother was, she may have also watched her cruelly separate families or use violence as a form of punishment. As a woman who formally held the title of slave owner, Jane Lanier Heard Allen was not powerless.[24]

Jane acquired ownership of at least 186 enslaved people after her husband passed away in 1853.[25] Her status as an enslaver brought on new responsibilities, including teaching Rebecca about the family business. Like men who shared knowledge of slaveholding with their sons, Jane taught her daughter similar lessons, which proved valuable when it was Rebecca's turn to lead.

While William Henry Mattox fought to protect the institution of slavery, Rebecca assumed control of their plantation and enslaved labor force. She was as invested in preserving their slaveholding empire as Mattox, having brought him a "goodly number of acres" when they married. He brought twenty-three enslaved laborers, seven mules, a horse, and at least a few of his own acres. Together, they built a thriving plantation in Elbert County, Georgia, where Rebecca lived not only as a plantation mistress but also as a landowning enslaver and woman of wealth and influence in her community.

In 1892, twenty-seven years after the end of chattel slavery, Rebecca reclaimed her status as a plantation mistress. The authority once associated with her role would continue, but there would be new limitations. She could no longer purchase enslaved laborers as before, not because they did not exist or she could not afford them, but because the criminal legal system now owned them and typically leased them only to white men. For a white woman to access forced labor, her husband or another male family member had to become a contracted lessee and then decide how much authority to delegate to her.

To clearly define the role of white women who owned land and leased prison labor—whether directly, through their husbands, or through other male family members—I am introducing the term "prison plantation mistress." This term captures several key traits of these women: they supported state-sanctioned slavery and participated in a system that allowed them to exploit Black prisoners; they aligned with their husbands and other prominent white men who profited from convict leasing; and they overlooked the system's inherent abuses for their own gain.

To be certain, prison plantation mistresses were not passive observers of convict leasing. They actively supported and condoned the practice, and Rebecca Mattox was no exception. Although William Henry Mattox held the lease, she benefited from the exploitation of the Black women he secured from the state: Nora Lay, Ella Gamble, Rose Henderson, Caroline Crittenden, Mollie Pierce, Hannah Holmes, Sarah Johnson, Emily Boone, Leila Burgess, Mollie Farmer, and dozens of others.

For seven years, the labor of these women provided for Rebecca. They cooked her meals, with food they had likely grown themselves, and labored so Rebecca could purchase the silk bonnets and Victorian-era dresses she proudly wore on the plantation—garments they could never afford, even if they had the right to wear them. Their labor may have also provided similar luxuries for her adult daughters, Annie and Carroll, who lived at Camp Heardmont as well.

As mistress of Camp Heardmont, Rebecca gained more than material comforts from exploiting Black women and likely played a role in managing them as well. In the household, she would have supervised the servants, possibly with help from her daughters. Her authority may well have extended beyond her neatly trimmed, boxwood-bordered walkways into the rugged quarters of the prison camp.

The full extent of Rebecca's responsibilities at Camp Heardmont remains unclear. One must wonder: In addition to overseeing the household, was she involved in managing the plantation's operations? If so, what would those duties have entailed? For instance, did she control the distribution of supplies to the women? Was she responsible for purchasing the fabric for their striped dresses or involved in decisions regarding their food? Did she determine when they would receive the occasional "good Sunday beef" or have power to exercise limitations that left them with the usual diet of pork, cornbread, and molasses? Would she have played a role in administering punishments or offering guidance to her husband about when to impose them? Or was "Cap'n Johnson," the guard, the only one allowed to crack the whip?

In 1899, William Henry Mattox's lease with the state of Georgia ended, and so did his prison plantation. Yet his memory persists, alongside other notable former enslavers who profited from prison labor: Joseph Emerson Brown and Elizabeth Grisham Brown, Zebulon Ward and Mary E. Worthen Ward, Arthur St. Clair Colyar and Agnes Erskine Estill Colyar, John Wallace Comer and Caroline Gertrude Seay, and General Nathan Bedford Forrest and Mary Ann Montgomery Forrest, among others.

The year 1883 marks a second emancipation for the Black women and men held captive on President's Island. That year, the "exiles" marched from Beal Street to the police station singing "Glory hallelujah!" behind a banner reading "President's Island Surrendered January, 1, 1883."[26] Once a refuge for the formerly enslaved, the island had been transformed into a site of forced labor. Black people on these lands went from owning it to living in fear of being trapped into convict leasing under the general of President's Island, Nathan Bedford Forrest.

While he is best known for cofounding the Ku Klux Klan and serving as its first national leader, Nathan Bedford Forrest also leased prisoners in the state of Tennessee. He started his career in the punishment industry as the owner of a slave jail in Memphis during the peak of the domestic slave trade. Although he is rarely compared to other prominent corporate-level traders, such as Isaac Franklin and John Armfield, he gained recognition as "one of the best known and richest slave-traders in all the South."[27]

After the Civil War, Forrest rebranded himself as a hirer of incarcerated labor, securing contracts with the state of Tennessee and the Shelby County Jail. To date, he remains the only known former slave trader and jailer to participate in convict leasing, as well as the only openly known Klansman to engage in the practice.

Black people arrested in Memphis feared being sent to Forrest's labor camp, aware of his reputation as one of the most vicious commanders of the Confederacy. "I ain't going to that work-house on President's Island; it might be like Fort Pillow," a group of Black prisoners boldly declared. They were "worked up into a fit over the prospect of being sent to Forrest's President's Island work-house."[28] They still remembered how General Forrest had led the massacre of approximately three hundred Black Union soldiers who should have been taken as prisoners of war. Now, eleven years later, he commanded Black prisoners in a different war—the War on Black Freedom.

In January 1875, Forrest began leasing prisoners from the state of Tennessee, taking possession of forty-five of them—seven women and thirty-eight men. The women who appear on the state's "List of Convicts at Work at General Forrest's" are Sarah (Sally) Ellis, Lou Wilson, Kate Harris, Mary Snyder, Sarah Lomax, Julia Reed, and Julia Warren. Unfortunately, the identities of those leased after 1875 remain unknown.[29]

A few months later, Forrest entered a five-year contract with Shelby County, gaining sole control of the county's jail and the two hundred prisoners who had been sentenced to "work out fines." He immediately put them to work on his 1,300-acre plantation, forcing them to clear and cultivate 550 acres of cotton and 250 acres of other crops, including corn, millet, Irish potatoes, and sweet potatoes.[30]

"We never had enough to eat," William Grant testified to a reporter for the *Daily Memphis Avalanche*. He was only sixteen when he was "sent down" to Forrest's camp for stealing two dollars the day after Christmas. "The rows was awful long," he described. If a person did not make it to the end with the others, they would get twenty-five lashes. He recalled the way "they whipped the women" for not keeping time.[31]

By May 5, 1876, Forrest gained possession of another 117 people: 60 Black males, 35 white males, 18 Black females, and four white females. This number excludes the "two Black women and ten Black men" he leased from the state.[32] Annie Porter spent six months on the island for "petit larceny." Kate Harris was held captive for "default of $10 fine and costs, for assaulting a colored sister."[33] As they worked their way off General Forrest's lands, the carceral system supplied him with more prisoners to take their place.

From what is evident in the historical record, Forrest gained about five new prisoners per day. This population growth is explained in monetary terms: "General Forrest gives to the county ten cents a day for all who are sent to him. This is a net gain, therefore, to the county of fifty cents a day." He also covered the cost of "turnkeys, gas, guards, and other expenses." Both Forrest and the county benefited from this arrangement: he gained hundreds of laborers and profits, while the county turned the misdemeanor docket from a "dead load to the tax-payers" into a "source of revenue."[34]

The people held captive by Nathan Bedford Forrest and Shelby County did not see themselves as a "dead load" or a "source of revenue" at all. They saw themselves as people with rights and took extreme measures to reclaim ownership over their lives: between July 1876 and January 1877 alone, seventy-four prisoners escaped from President's Island.[35] Forrest explained the escapes from his camp in a letter to Honorable Tom Holman, chairman of the county court in Memphis: "The number of escapes is large, but that is owing mostly to the facilities afforded them by the negro population on the island, and the large amount of undergrowth on the island." He also reassured Holman, "As I have now got rid of most of the negro residents, and have my lands nearly all cleared up, I feel confident that the proportion of escapes will hereafter be much less."[36] But the people kept running.

Pink Walker took flight not long after landing on the island. She was rearrested on the mainland in Memphis, where most people fled, and sent back to "work out a fifty-dollar fine and costs." It appears that the judge added to her punishment by levying an additional fine against her for stealing her freedom.[37]

As a community, the prisoners of President's Island grew tired of being subjected to the "thud of the big black strap, and piteous wail of anguish; of hard work, from early dawn until darkness; of food often unfit to be eaten; of a lifetime's sufferings crowded into weeks."[38] There was only one thing left to do—burn the island down to take back their freedom.

In December 1877, shortly after the death of Nathan Bedford Forrest, his widow, Mary Ann Montgomery Forrest, and their son, William Forrest, took control of the family's convict lease farm. Less than two months later, the prisoners set fire to it. "Numbering near a hundred, [they] took possession of the island to burn down everything on it and escape to the woods on one side or the other," one newspaper reported. The rebellion ended with only a few buildings destroyed, but it restored the prisoners' dignity and sent a clear message that they would no longer tolerate the abuses they had suffered.[39]

At the time of the uprising, Mary Forrest owned the convict labor camp, while her son and business partner, "Captain Willie," oversaw its operations. She was not only the administrator of the plantation on President's Island but also a key figure in managing the business and finances—skills she likely developed during her previous experience as an enslaver in Mississippi. Her marriage to a prominent enslaver, slave trader, and owner of a slave jail would have also exposed her to insights into the business of slavery, which she effectively applied to the leasing of prisoners.

In January 1878, the county leased the Shelby County workhouse "to the widow of Gen. Forrest for five years." But before the deal was finalized, Mary had to agree to pay the remaining balance on her late husband's contract—$3,000. By January 1880, she and William secured an additional contract to lease prisoners from Tipton County, and they later gained authorization to lease district prisoners as well.[40] Under Mary's leadership, the family's punishment business grew, as did the number of Black women held on President's Island.

In May 1878, Kate Jackson, Lacey Harris, and Belle Watkins were sent to President's Island together. Kate received a two-year sentence for assault, Lacey was sentenced to fourteen months for vagrancy, and Belle was given thirty days for larceny. They were joined by at least six other Black women serving time for similar "crimes."[41]

While the Forrest family worked to keep Black women confined, the women fought for their freedom. On May 7, 1878, Julia Higgins escaped from President's Island by swimming eight miles to Memphis. What happened next is unclear; no records show whether she remained free or was returned to the island by authorities. What is evident, however, is that the Black women prisoners were determined not to be held captive on Mary's lands. They preferred to face the consequences of seeking their freedom than remain in chains.[42]

The brutality of President's Island continued to make headlines in the years following General Forrest's death. Grand juries were sent to investigate conditions on the farm, uncovering grisly stories of violence and even death—several prisoners had been murdered there. The abuses mounted, and so did the lawsuits. In 1880, prisoners leased to Mary Forrest filed $91,500 in claims against her and William, alleging "cruel and inhuman treatment."[43]

Critics compared the abuses on President's Island to the brutality of Simon Legree, the slaveholder in Harriet Beecher Stowe's *Uncle Tom's Cabin*. Investigations into the convict labor camp confirmed these claims, raising enough concern to lead to its eventual closure. After eight long years, Shelby County ended its contract with the Forrest family, as did the other entities they worked with. When Mary's lease expired on January 1, 1883, it brought convict leasing on President's Island to an end—a long-awaited victory for those who had been held captive there.

By the turn of the twentieth century, convict leasing began to decline across the South. Its economic profitability gradually decreased as shifts in the economy made the system less attractive and sustainable. Although convict leasing initially provided a cost-effective solution for modernizing the South, it became increasingly expensive. Lessees ended up with more laborers than they needed—laborers they were contractually obligated to keep—since they could not dismiss them and had to pay the fixed costs regardless of economic conditions. Other factors contributed to the system's collapse, including competition from free labor, rising public pressure, shifting political landscapes, and national outrage over its inhumanity, driven by progressive reformers.

The plight of women, primarily Black women who made up most of the system's female prisoners, became a major concern among progressive reformers eager to abolish convict leasing. Reformers, both Black and white, criticized its impact on these women but for different reasons. Black women activists, such as Mary Church Terrell, viewed the system as a crueler form of slavery: "It is perfectly clear, therefore, that it is no exaggeration to say that in some respects the convict lease system . . . is less humane than was the bondage endured by slaves fifty years ago," she expressed.[44] Her efforts to abolish the system stemmed from a desire to protect Black women and the race from its violent abuses.

White women activists voiced similar concerns about the system's impact on imprisoned women and the *white* race. White men's assaults on Black women resulted in mixed-race children, which were seen as a stain on their race. By abolishing convict leasing, they hoped to prevent the spread of "miscegenation," which they believed undermined white women's roles as mothers and wives.

The incarceration of Black women spurred the creation of state-run prison farms in the South. In the absence of reformatories like those established for white women prisoners in the North, Black women were put to work. In this region, the system never intended to rehabilitate them. The removal of Black women from convict lease camps was not for their protection but solely to generate profit. This early exploitation of Black women's labor on state-owned lands generated income to construct buildings, hire staff, and support the state's male prisoners.

The state of Georgia exemplifies how state prison systems exploited Black women to generate wealth. In 1899, the state legislature passed a law requiring that all women prisoners with felony convictions transfer to the state's prison farm in Milledgeville. Seventy-three Black women, most previously held by private investors, continued picking cotton on publicly owned land. Their labor produced 454,500 pounds of cotton for the state in the first four years of the farm's operation, earning more than $30,000 in profit.[45]

The four white women prisoners at the farm did not work in the fields alongside Black women, nor did they participate in the building of state-owned lands for profit. The same is true for most white women incarcerated across the South, a region that, though technically classifying them as state property, did not view them as commodities.

Although confined within the same systems that oppressed Black women, white women did not experience its effects equally. Jane Crow's inequality shielded them from brutal labor and punishment. But every now and then, white men, like Warden Allagood, tested the boundaries of white women's racial privilege.

"The whipping of Miss DeCris is a blot on the South. Every man with any manhood in his soul should rise up and demand justice for the girl. The white women of the south especially must be protected and every honor that can be thrown around them should be given," reflected the sentiment of white women and men familiar with Mamie DeCris's case. Mamie, a white woman—not a "girl"—told her story to the press in August 1903, drawing national attention to Georgia's prison system.[46]

"I refused warden's advances, told of them, and he lashed me," Mamie claimed. "Before this, I had many privileges. . . . These were afterwards all denied me."[47] The warden admitted to whipping Mamie for "insubordination," while denying claims that he made sexual advances toward her. He also admitted to giving her a "taste of the work in the field," telling the guard to "work her easily; . . . to let her rest whenever she wanted to, but keeping her steady enough at work to awake her to a realization of the privileges she was enjoying in the house."[48]

While Mamie's case drew great interest, the struggles of Black women remained largely unnoticed. Their daily lives continued as before, marked by grueling labor, harsh punishment, and countless injustices on the farm. Yet amid these struggles, Black women found hope. Their faith became the soundtrack of their lives, captured in rare recordings by folklorist John Avery Lomax at the Georgia State Prison Farm. In these recordings, Black women express their longings for deliverance, family, and freedom through song.

Some verses raise hopes:

I'm down in trouble,
waitin' on you
waitin' on you
waitin' on you
We down in trouble,
waitin' on you
I can't do nothin' til you come

Other verses encourage happiness:

I have a mother,
at the beautiful gate
at the beautiful gate
at the beautiful gate
I have a mother,
at the beautiful gate
She's a waitin' and watchin' for me

Like generations of women before them, Black women sang their way to freedom, holding fast to the hope of God's rescue from bondage and the joy of reunion with lost kin. They hummed, hollered, laughed, cried, prayed, clapped, and shouted their way through every state-run plantation in America, including Angola Plantation in Louisiana, Parchman Farm in Mississippi, Goree State Farm in Texas, Eastham Prison Farm in Texas, Cummins State Farm in Arkansas, and Raiford Prison Farm in Florida. They transformed cotton rows into choir rows, creating worlds for themselves beyond the punitive realm imposed by the state. In their world, they were people, not property; citizens, not slaves; survivors, not criminals.[49]

Mass incarceration for profit originated in the South but now impacts every region of the United States. The War on Drugs, initiated in the early 1970s, turned for-profit punishment from a regional issue into a nationwide crisis.[50] Throughout this time, Black women have continued to bear its disproportionate effects.

Although Black women make up only 15.3 percent of America's female population today, they represent 17 percent of its female prison population.[51] This marks a significant decrease from the peak years of the 1980s and 1990s, when the incarceration rate for Black women soared by a staggering 828 percent.[52] Until the turn of the twentieth-first century, this trend persisted, resulting in Black women being imprisoned at a rate 7.5 times higher than white women. Today, the United States remains the world leader in women's incarceration—a title resulting from the War on Drugs and its devastating impact on Black women.[53]

The present-day mass incarceration of Black women can be traced to the expansion of the Drug War in the 1980s and 1990s. However, as this book argues, the crisis of imprisonment for Black women goes back much further, with its origins in slavery, the resulting War on Black Freedom, and the long-standing effects of Jane Crow's inequalities. Exploring these historical roots helps situate the War on Drugs as the final chapter in this history, not the first. It also provides context for the growth of the profit-driven prison system, which has expanded drastically since 1865.

While this chapter has primarily focused on the role of public prisons and private industry in driving the mass incarceration epidemic in the past, private prisons have played an equally vital role in sustaining the for-profit punishment industry today. Beginning in the 1980s, billion-dollar corporations such as Corrections Corporation of America (now CoreCivic) and Geo Group began building private prisons. Increased overcrowding in state and federal prisons created financial opportunities for these companies; as the prison population grew due to the War on Drugs, so did the demand for carceral facilities.

Private prisons were marketed as a solution to a problem of over-punishment but became a major driver of mass incarceration. As Michelle Alexander notes in *The New Jim Crow*, the private prison boom of the 1980s and 1990s dangerously accelerated incarceration rates for Black Americans. Although it was not the sole force behind the system, private prisons have financially incentivized punishment in ways reminiscent of the post-Emancipation era.

Private prison companies profit from constructing their own facilities and acquiring state and federal prisons. Their business model relies on maximizing profits through government contracts, as they receive payments for each prisoner in their custody. This creates an incentive to maintain high occupancy rates: more prisoners mean higher profits.

In 2012, Corrections Corporation of America (CCA), the nation's largest operator of for-profit prisons, sent a letter to forty-eight states offering to buy their prisons as part of its "corrections investment initiative." "CCA is earmarking $250 million for purchasing and managing government-owned corrections facilities," wrote former CCA executive vice president and chief corrections officer Harley G. Lappin. Emphasizing CCA's mission of delivering "private-sector excellence by constructing and managing new corrections facilities for our government partners," he articulated CCA's mission to expand its power over state property, including the people owned by the state.[54] While, ultimately, the company's plan to take over America's punishment industry failed, this example illustrates the persistence of public-private partnerships and profit-based punishment that has prevailed for centuries.

In 2024, CoreCivic reported a revenue of $2.0 billion, with a net income of $68.9 million. The company predicts it will earn a net income of $53.5 million to $67.5 million in 2025. Its competitor, Geo Group, had a total revenue of $2.42 billion in 2024, and a net income of $31.9 million.[55]

Although private prison corporations continue to earn profits in the billions, they are building fewer private prisons, pivoting instead toward facilities to detain immigrants. This shift stems from public protests and pressure to end mass incarceration, as well as declining investment from banks that once financed the expansion of the twentieth-century for-profit prison boom—Wells Fargo, Bank of America, SunTrust, Barclays, and Fifth Third, to name a few. *Many of these same banks provided financing for chattel slavery in the nineteenth century*. Instead of building new prisons (aside from immigration detention facilities), they now primarily manage existing ones. Today, twenty-seven states and the federal government rely on private corporations like the GEO Group and CoreCivic to run their correctional facilities.[56]

Today, the nation's public prison system generates an estimated $74 billion a year.[57] Yet this pales in comparison to the profits earned by the four thousand-plus companies involved in the punishment industry. These businesses represent nearly every aspect of the private sector, including food and commissary services, transportation, technology, communications, security, building construction, financial services, data management, security and surveillance, healthcare, and even education. Some of the nation's largest retailers and corporations have historically been part of this system, including Victoria's Secret, BP, McDonald's, Wendy's, Burger King, Coca-Cola, Cargill, Kroger, Whole Foods, Target, Walmart, Home Depot, Starbucks, Verizon, FamilySearch, Hyundai, Avis, Kmart, and JCPenney, to name a few.[58]

Prisoners are also exploited for profit and public gain in ways that are rarely mentioned. Food grown on prison plantations helps produce some of the nation's most popular food brands. Office furniture made by incarcerated people supports state institutions and universities, contributing to higher education. And even though imprisoned people are no longer forced to produce personal protective equipment for the COVID-19 pandemic, it is important to acknowledge their role in providing lifesaving PPE—equipment they themselves were not allowed to use. Their labor in protecting the nation redefines what it means to be an essential worker.

Although prisoner labor benefits companies and institutions, most often it is exploited for the operation of the prisons themselves. Prisons rely on incarcerated people to perform field work, factory labor, food service, laundry, and other essential jobs. While most states pay between 86 cents and $3.45 per day for this work, the former slave states of Arkansas, Alabama, Texas, Florida, Georgia, Mississippi, and South Carolina pay nothing.[59]

Throughout history—and even today—private companies and individuals have profited from prison labor, while incarcerated individuals and their families have suffered losses that cannot be measured in dollars. The human cost of punishment far exceeds the debt this cruel practice owes its victims.[60]

For Black women, being trapped in America's profit-driven prison system has carried enormous social costs. It has meant losing access to freedom, citizenship rights, employment, education, safe housing, and family connections. It has also meant having children taken away by the state and placed for adoption under laws like the Adoption and Safe Families Act, which turned child "welfare" into a modern-day auction block at the height of the War on Drugs. Profit-driven prisons not only generate income for private investors but also reinforce a centuries-long epidemic of family separation. From the domestic slave trade to the War on Drugs, family separation and for-profit incarceration have been inseparably linked.

CHAPTER 5

FAMILY SEPARATION

Stephanie vividly remembered the day her daughter was born. She came out with "a head full of hair, chubby cheeks, and big ole eyes," Stephanie recalled. "It was an amazing feeling." It was the kind of feeling mothers get when they meet their babies for the first time, no matter their race, financial condition, or freedom status. Though on probation at the time, Stephanie gave birth feeling no less attached to or proud of what she had accomplished. Her baby girl gave her renewed purpose and a reason to keep getting her life together, though she did not realize it would all soon fall apart.

"I was holding her, and they came in and took her," Stephanie remembered. A group of Child Protective Services (CPS) social workers seized Stephanie's daughter the day after she was born. The little bed where she lay next to her mother suddenly disappeared as the newborn was taken into custody. First jailed in the hospital nursery, then in an emergency foster care placement, Stephanie's baby was treated as if she had committed a crime.

"They had a lady come and get her," Stephanie shared. For an entire weekend, she searched frantically for her baby before learning she had been placed with a kind-spirited woman who allowed Stephanie to see her. As the court decided on whether her baby would be released from state custody, Stephanie settled for short visits with her at Target and other places in their California town.[1] But then Stephanie got arrested on a warrant, which violated her probation.

For the next couple of years, she would receive additional violations for missing in-person check-ins with her probation officer. Unfortunately, she did not have access to a car. It is sobering to realize how something as ordinary as a lack of transportation can lead to a person being violated and sent back to jail or prison.

Stephanie managed to get rides to the CPS agency to try to set up visitations with her daughter—her "little mini me," as she called her—but the social worker never returned her calls. This led to her missing numerous court-ordered visitations. Her perceived absence from her daughter's life left a negative impression on the judge, who ruled Stephanie unfit to care for the baby she had carried for nine months. It did not matter that she had spent the first year and a half of her baby's life navigating the child "welfare" system while a stranger experienced the joy of watching her take her first steps. The system did not see her as a loving mother doing her best but as someone who did not deserve to be a mother at all. By January 2018, Stephanie's journey as a mother came to a brutal end. A judge terminated her parental rights.

Stephanie was in jail on a probation violation when she got the news. The child support order against her had suddenly disappeared, raising immediate red flags. The state had been billing her for payments it had made while fostering her child. In the US, when a child enters foster care, the custodial parent is required to pay child support to the state. Seeing a zero balance next to her name forced her to face a grim reality: her child had been adopted out, so she was no longer required to pay child support.

The news hit Stephanie hard. "I felt hopeless," she recalled. Her despair echoed across three centuries, exposing the feelings of enslaved women who carried similar grief and love in their hearts for their missing children. "You can never understand the slave mother's emotions as she clasps her new-born child, and knows that a master's word can at any moment take it from her embrace," Bethany Veney lamented after losing her daughter Charlotte in the domestic slave trade.[2] Bethany was in a slave jail while her enslaver decided the fate of her daughter—a daughter she would never see again.

This is where the past meets the present: Stephanie sat in jail on a probation violation while her baby was being prepared for adoption. She had no idea what was happening as her baby's foster "mom" packed up her favorite toys, blankets, and other belongings for her new permanent home. "I was county property," Stephanie said, comparing her situation to that of an enslaved mother. Before reaching her second birthday, Stephanie's baby was put up for adoption through a modern-day auction block—the Adoption and Safe Families Act.

The Adoption and Safe Families Act (ASFA) was signed into law by President Bill Clinton on November 19, 1997, just three years after the ratification of the 1994 Clinton Crime Bill, the largest federal crime legislation in US history. Like the Fugitive Slave Act—America's first major federal crime bill—the Crime Bill exacerbated the growth of a mass incarceration epidemic, resulting in a sharp increase in Black incarceration rates for nonviolent drug "crimes." Furthermore, it catalyzed the growth of a racially charged child "welfare" system; as more Black mothers and fathers entered prison, more Black children entered state custody.

When ASFA took effect, roughly 560,000 children were in foster care, the majority of them Black. Although Black children comprised only 15 percent of the nation's total child population in 1997, they represented approximately 41 percent of the child "welfare" population.[3] Their numbers nearly parallel incarceration rates of Black women during this period, pointing to a stark conclusion: the War on Drugs made the United States not only the global leader in incarceration but also a world leader in family separation.

As Black mothers entered the prison system in record numbers, so did their children enter into the foster care system. This is an often overlooked aspect of the mass incarceration story: the correlation between the imprisonment of Black women and the influx of Black children into the child "welfare" system. The Adoption and Safe Families Act was created as a "solution" to this surge, but it undeniably worsened the family separation epidemic for Black families. This explains my use of the term "auction block" to describe ASFA, a law that not only perpetuates slavery's legacy of family separation but turns innocent children into state property.

Stephanie's baby was adopted for a payment of around $5,000 made to the state of California by the federal government. This was the standard rate for an able-bodied child her age that year. Children with "special needs" or those older than nine drew larger financial incentives—up to a $6,000 "super-bonus."[4]

In 2018, the state of California received approximately $7,715,000 for the 6,966 children it adopted out, including Stephanie's daughter. It may seem shocking, but family separation is as prevalent in the United States today as it was over two hundred years ago. In fact, since ASFA was signed into law, more Black children have been trafficked through foster care and public adoptions than were separated from their families during the domestic slave trade.[5] You read that correctly: as of this book's writing in 2025—less than thirty years later—it has already caused more Black children to be separated from their families than during the domestic slave trade.

This chapter begins by exploring the roots of Black family separation during the first era of mass incarceration: the domestic slave trade. It traces its effects on enslaved, incarcerated, and free Black mothers, emphasizing the profound impact of family loss—an impact that persisted long after 1865. In the aftermath of freedom, Black families were reunited *and* separated, legally restored *and* dismantled. Some parents lost their children to the apprenticeship system under the Black Codes, which permitted former enslavers to claim custodial rights over Black children. Others lost them while serving time in jail, on chain gangs, in fixed-term slavery arrangements, in debt peonage farms, or in profit-driven prison systems such as convict leasing and state-owned prison plantations. A century later, the criminal legal system continued tearing apart Black families through the War on Drugs and the Adoption and Safe Families

Act, leaving more children without their parents than during the chattel slavery era.

"My son, as yonder leaves are stripped from off the trees of the forest, so are the children of the slaves swept away from them by the hands of cruel tyrants," Henry "Box" Brown's mother would say, as "tears would find their way down her saddened cheeks." Then she would press him into her "heaving bosom," as if to save him from "so dreaded a calamity, or to feast on the enjoyments of maternal feeling while she yet retained possession of her child."[6] As Henry grew older, the threat of loss became ever more imminent, until the time came for them to say good-bye.

"My feelings were very much tried by the separation which I had thus to endure. . . . I began to feel, indeed, that I really was alone in the world," Henry remembered. Eventually, he grew into a man and married Nancy. They had children, a little house of their own, and a lot of love for twelve years. "I felt that life had joys worth living for," he recalled. Then, like the leaves of the forest of which his mother warned, Henry's entire family was swept away into the domestic slave trade.

"I had not been many hours at my work, when I was informed that my wife and children were taken from their home, sent to the auction mart and sold, and then lay in prison [jail] ready to start away the next day for North Carolina with the man who had purchased them," Henry stated. "I went and purchased some things to take to the jail to them I so much loved; and to have one farewell embrace before parting for ever."[7]

Henry never made it to the jail, having been warned that if he stepped inside, he would be incarcerated and sold. So he ultimately said his good-byes from the side of a street. "I . . . had the melancholy satisfaction of witnessing the approach of a gang of slaves, amounting to three hundred and fifty in number, marching under the direction of a methodist minister, by whom they were purchased, and amongst which slaves were my wife and children," he lamented. "This train of beings was accompanied by a number of waggons [*sic*] loaded with little children of many different families . . . but what should I now see in the very foremost waggon but a little child looking towards me and pitifully calling, father! father! This was my eldest child, and I was obliged to look upon it for the last time that I should, perhaps, ever see it again in life."[8]

About half of all enslaved individuals faced family separation like Henry, with one in four of these being children.[9] Enslaved parents like Henry and Nancy had no legal rights over their children, who could be sold without notice. This reality hit Black mothers especially hard since they often served as primary caregivers for their young—children they did not legally possess.

Being an enslaved woman foreclosed any legal possibility of becoming a mother. Every child she gave birth to belonged to her enslaver. But the law could not control her love for her babies. Only an enslaved woman could choose the expanse of her love, and even the deep void of grief borne by family separation could not diminish it.

In 1852, an enslaved mother named Rose, on the day she was sold away from her nine-year-old daughter Ashley, gave her a cotton sack. Inside, she placed an old dress, three handfuls of pecans, and a lock of her own hair, telling her it was "filled with my love always." Ashley never saw her mother again, but she continued to carry her mother's sack of love.[10]

Laura showed her love in a different way. Rather than giving her children material gifts, she gave them a chance to become free. On October 10, 1856, she packed their belongings and they fled together. Unfortunately, the family did not get far before being arrested and taken to jail in Washington, DC. For 254 days, Laura anxiously awaited a decision from the circuit court regarding her fate and that of her two young children. Then, in a brutal judgment, the court ordered the sheriff to auction them off to cover their jail fees, which amounted to $262.08.[11]

There is no doubt enslaved mothers loved their children, despite inconsistent bonds. For some, these bonds were close. For others, they were distant or nonexistent; it would be naive to assume that every enslaved woman desired motherhood. Living with the knowledge that one's child would become the property of an enslaver and endure the abuses of slavery, including family separation, surely inflicted greater pain than even childbirth.

Despite their circumstances, mothers and children defined their relationships on their own terms, even as the law dictated their identity. Long before the United States officially became a nation, it was decided that a Black child's freedom status would be contingent on the status of its mother. In 1662, Virginia became the first colony to make slavery inheritable. Other colonies that later became states followed suit, establishing a legal precedent that has plagued Black mothers for centuries.

The earliest instance of Jane Crow's inequality appears in seventeenth-century "womb laws" that governed Black motherhood. These laws established that children born to enslaved mothers would automatically be enslaved, while children born to free Black mothers would be legally recognized as free. Establishing a system of racial slavery based on heritability was essential in the process of severing Black family bonds. As historian Jennifer L. Morgan powerfully explains: "Enslaved people had to be understood as dispossessed, outside of the normal networks of family and community, to justify the practice of mass enslavement."[12]

During the era of chattel slavery, free Black mothers and their children lived on the margins of typical family and community networks. As second-class free people, they did not possess the same family security as white citizens; Black people had legal freedom but no citizenship rights. The freedom of Black mothers was often limited, directly affecting their rights to motherhood. Even a seemingly minor violation—not carrying freedom papers or failing to register their status with the courts, a burden that white mothers never faced—could lead to family separation through incarceration or enslavement. Poverty was another significant factor that caused Black mothers to lose custody of their children.

So, what happened to the children left behind? Most were placed in a system known as "apprenticeship." This legal arrangement bound children to a "master" for their labor through contracts supervised by Orphans'

Courts. In exchange, they were promised benefits such as housing, clothing, food, training in a skill or trade, and, for white children, an education.

The apprenticeship system can be viewed as an early form of child welfare, initially established to support impoverished white children. It was only after 1865 that the system became explicitly racialized through the Black Codes. Before then, it functioned much like today's foster care system, placing orphans, poor children, and others considered unable to be supported by their families under the custody of an adult until they reached legal age, typically twenty-one for boys and sixteen for girls.

The apprenticeship system affected children of both races, but its impact on Black children was worsened by chattel slavery. Free Black children often experienced this system as a form of forced labor, as they were frequently apprenticed to white "masters" against their will. This involuntary apprenticeship perpetuated the conditions of slavery for free Black children and contributed to family separations across the entire Black community, both enslaved and free.[13]

In the American South, as well as in some northern cities with large populations of free Black residents, such as Philadelphia, free Black children were often forced into involuntary apprenticeships. This could happen if their parents were considered vagrants or if local courts determined that the children were not being raised in a "proper manner."[14] Failing to provide work exposure or "suitable" employment opportunities—usually under white supervision—could also lead to forced family separation. To be clear, Black children were routinely orphaned by the courts, not because their parents died or left them, but because their parents were deemed "unfit" to raise them.

In the state of Maryland, which had the largest free Black population in the United States, Orphans' Court judges had the legal authority to bind out "any child or children of free negroes or mulattoes not at service or learning a trade, or employed in the service of their parents."[15] Trustees of the poor and justices of the peace could also "issue a citation to the sheriff or any constable of the county, to cause to be brought before them . . . the child or children of lazy, indolent, and worthless free negroes, and bind them out as apprentices."[16]

Augusta Spriggs was one of many free Black children forced into apprenticeship. Her story shows how deeply racialized this system was and how closely it mirrored slavery: Augusta was treated more like an enslaved person than as an individual with legal freedom. As a second-class free child without citizenship, she was at the mercy of the court system, which involuntarily bound her to four white "masters."

Augusta's ordeal started in October 1849, when the Trustees of the Poor of Baltimore City and County bound her to a local white man named Joseph Merryman. At thirteen, she was placed in his cold and unsettling care, far from her mother's embrace. For three years, she worked as his servant before finally gaining her freedom by running away.

Augusta was eventually captured and imprisoned in the Baltimore City Jail. Merryman paid five dollars for her release, but she escaped again twenty-four hours later, costing him an additional two dollars. Realizing Augusta would never submit to him, he petitioned the Orphans' Court for Baltimore County to sell her unexpired term of twelve months. The court granted his request, and on August 31, 1852, Augusta was sold to David H. White.[17]

White bought Augusta's labor for an undisclosed amount, exploiting her until she ended his power over her: she ran. For eighteen months, he searched in vain as she hid out in the city, possibly reuniting with her mother and reclaiming the love taken from her by her captors and the court system. Or maybe not. Given the high rates of incarceration for free Black women accused of vagrancy and other petty crimes, it is possible that Augusta's mother was incarcerated, or worse, enslaved. If so, the Orphans' Court would have had the legal right to claim her daughter.

But Augusta refused to be claimed by anyone. After incurring "great expense" searching for her, David White finally tracked her down and recouped his losses from the court by selling her to James S. Wilson.

By the time Wilson acquired her in April 1856, Augusta had aged out of the apprenticeship system. Her adulthood was made apparent in a runaway advertisement published by him in the *Sun* newspaper: "$50 DOLLARS REWARD. Ran away from the subscriber on the 18th day of June last, a MULATTO GIRL named 'Augusta Jane Spriggs'; twenty years of age . . . I will give the above reward if brought home or secured so that I can get her."[18] Like Merryman and White, Wilson paid a hefty price for having Augusta repeatedly captured and imprisoned for refusing to be his slave. And, like the others, he succeeded in getting the Orphans' Court to sell her, this time to an enslaver.

On December 27, 1856, three judges approved Wilson's petition. They authorized the "sale and transfer" of Augusta to Alfred B. Berry, a prominent slave owner in Prince George's County, Maryland, until October 24, 1860—an additional four years. While this imposed an unprecedented injustice against her, it was perfectly legal. An 1839 law governing Black apprentices gave the court "full power to authorize the master of such absconding [Negro] apprentice to sell such apprentice to any person within this State," which included an enslaver.[19]

Over nearly ten years, Augusta went from being held captive by the court system and three different "masters" to being forced to work on a slave plantation, even though she was legally free. It was a harrowing experience for her; as a free person, she never expected to endure the perils of chattel slavery. But there she was, working among twenty-eight enslaved laborers—thirteen adults and fifteen children—until she freed herself by running away.[20]

After being committed to the Howard County Jail on April 2, 1857, for pursuing her freedom, the county sheriff published an advertisement announcing Augusta's detainment. He also issued a warning: "if the said Negress is not claimed within sixty days she will be liberated according to law." The sheriff thus acknowledged Augusta's legal right to freedom, a right she had demanded since the court system had taken it away.[21]

It is unclear whether Augusta ever gained her freedom. The same uncertainty surrounds the countless free Black children exploited by

Maryland's Orphans' Courts due to poverty, death, voluntary abandonment, and court-enforced family separation. Even less is known about the free Black children born in prison who were subsequently forced into apprenticeships.

In 1814, the Maryland state legislature gave penitentiary inspectors the authority to bind as apprentices "the children of female convicts, born during their times of service, the males until twenty-one, and females until sixteen years of age."[22] This law was passed when free Black women made up most of Maryland's female prison population. Between 1812 and 1860, Black women represented almost 70 percent of the state's female prisoners—667 of the 953 women admitted to the Maryland State Penitentiary.[23]

One cannot help but wonder how this law uniquely affected Black mothers and their children. Did it foreshadow the consequences of the ASFA bill nearly two hundred years later by stripping incarcerated mothers of their parental rights and turning their children into sources of profit? Did it establish a historical precedent for the treatment of children born in prison? And did it shape the future for Black children born into the system, who, by law, inherited their mother's status as state property?

The answers remain buried in the past. But it is evident the apprenticeship system further entrenched Black family separation, including for those experiencing incarceration. It gave white "masters" long-term access to incarcerated women's children who, unlike other apprenticed children, had no legal rights. Essentially wards of the state, these children could be held in the system long after their mothers were released from prison, gaining freedom only when they reached the legal age.

After the end of chattel slavery, Black mothers gained parental rights for the first time in American history. The Thirteenth Amendment not only abolished chattel slavery but also ended the ownership that white people had over their children. At last, Black women could realize the long-held dream of giving birth to free children they could keep. They could also celebrate that every child born from their womb would enter the world as a legally recognized human being.

These renewed hopes touched all Black mothers, including those who had experienced both the joy and heartbreak of motherhood during chattel slavery. They tirelessly searched for the children they had lost, placing "Information Wanted" advertisements in newspapers and relying on word of mouth. Their desperation is well-documented in the ads recovered by the Last Seen project, which chronicles the struggle of formerly enslaved people to find their lost loved ones.[24]

Mrs. Mattie spent decades searching for her missing child. On January 24, 1907, she published what might have been one of many pleas made throughout the years. This one was short and straightforward: "Any news concerning the whereabouts of Emma, the daughter of Mrs. Mattie . . . will be eagerly welcomed by her mother," she wrote.[25]

Formerly enslaved children also never gave up on finding their missing mothers. Joe Slatton spent forty-four years searching for his, even on Christmas Day 1909. "I am in search of my mother, Rosie Ingram. Last heard from had two children, named Joe and Mary. Joe was taken from her," he wrote in his advertisement for "Lost Relatives."[26]

While most searches proved unsuccessful, some individuals did manage to find loved ones. Aggie and Levi, a married couple, found each other forty years after slavery severed their bond. Their love story was short but sweet—they met at a dance in 1844, married in 1847, and were separated in 1848. Though many years had passed, they carried an "aching void in their lives." Each moved on, marrying new partners and raising lots of children. Then death took their spouses away, bringing the pair back together; a few months after his wife died, Levi "went for" Aggie. She joyfully reunited with her first love, reigniting a romance that had been cut short before it could fully begin.[27]

As Black families found their way back to one another, the legal system found new ways to keep them apart. State-sponsored Black Codes helped reignite the Black family separation epidemic through race-based apprenticeship laws, vagrancy laws, and other discriminatory legislation that stripped Black people of their freedom and their families. Even after gaining legal freedom and citizenship rights, Black people still lacked protections for their family bonds.

The apprenticeship system was a key component of the Black Codes, discriminatory laws enacted in the South after the Civil War to restrict the rights of newly freed Black people. Under this system, state authorities could bind Black children to white employers without parental consent. Much like during chattel slavery, this system separated children from parents deemed too poor or "unfit" to care for them. In the earliest days of freedom, when Black family bonds were still tenuous, Orphans' Courts doubled down on their efforts to terminate the parental rights of formerly enslaved mothers and fathers, placing their sons and daughters in the legal custody of former slaveholders who had owned them.[28]

"Dear Daughter Leathe . . . they have took Dorra child and bound it out to Miss Sally Husband tell she is twenty one . . . i had her a good home but they come and took her away and then had her bound to him," wrote Aima Shipp in May 1866.[29] Aima's granddaughter, Louisa, had been involuntarily bound to the son-in-law of her former enslaver, William M. Shipp, despite Dora's dying wish for her mother, Aima, and her sister Lethia ("Leathe") to gain custody of her children.

Lethia hired an attorney and gave a sworn statement before a justice of the peace in Christian County, Kentucky, where her niece was being confined. When William M. Shipp learned of this, he became enraged: "The peticion gotten up . . . in Behalf of a dirty negro wench that I once owned by the name of Lethy." However, Lethia pressed on, defying his authority until an investigation showed that her niece had not been legally bound.

Meanwhile, Louisa refused to wait for a court to grant her freedom. She "ran off" to her aunt Lethia, hoping it would be the last time she would have to escape. However, Louisa's quest ended as suddenly as it had begun, leaving Louisa in bondage and her aunt arrested.

Louisa's story reflects the experiences of thousands of Black children forced into apprenticeships after the Civil War. Most endured court-ordered indentures whereby an individual, usually a former enslaver, took possession of a child after petitioning the courts. Black mothers who intervened risked imprisonment or violent attacks.

On March 27, 1866, a Black mother was "sentenced to be sold" as a fixed-term slave for two years for encouraging her children to leave their former enslaver, who had apprenticed them without her consent. To support themselves after their planned escape, the children had even secured paid employment totaling $400 per year. However, their former enslaver had already devised his own plans to make them work for free.[30]

On November 29, 1866, Eliza Smith's daughter, Olivia, was also "taken from her by force" and apprenticed to a former enslaver named John S. Armiger in Huntingtown, Maryland. Mr. and Mrs. Basil Crowdy's three children were bound out too, "not withstanding the protest of both parents." Although the Crowdys went to court after being summoned and "steadily refused to consent to the binding," the judge refused to restore their parental rights. Mrs. Crowdy would not take no for an answer, and as a result, was punished with violence. "The Constable A. O. Buckmunslin finding the mother obdurate struck her in the face with his fist in the presence of the judges."[31]

Black mothers consistently risked their lives, safety, and personal freedom for the sake of their children. At times, they confronted racist judges or faced off against their former enslavers. Despite their limited rights, Black women discovered ways to legally advocate for their children's freedom.

On May 6, 1865, Leah Coston petitioned the Criminal Court of Baltimore city for a writ of habeas corpus against her former enslaver, Samuel Coston, "commanding him to produce before said Court the bodies of Simon and Washington Coston." According to the boys' mother, Coston had "illegally arrested" and held them in custody. Samuel Coston maintained that he held legal rights to her infant children, refusing to give them up.[32]

The ratification of the 1864 Maryland Constitution, which ended chattel slavery in the state, left enslavers like Samuel Coston scrambling for cheap labor. Their solution: bind out Black children. Leah's babies joined an estimated three to four thousand Black minors in Maryland forced into labor contracts as apprentices beginning in 1864.[33] They also joined an undocumented number of children who were illegally bound while legally enslaved.

In her petition to the court, Leah detailed Coston's unlawful actions, which included apprenticing her children while they were still enslaved to him. He had acquired permission from the Orphans' Court of Somerset County, Maryland, to bind the children *before* the ratification of the new state constitution. Because Leah was never summoned to the binding, she had no chance to explain the illegality of Coston's actions. Her absence from court affected the judge's perception of her; he interpreted it as a lack of interest in the welfare of her children, whom he believed to be free. Unaware that she was enslaved, the judge punished Leah as if she were a free Black mother, forcing her sons to be apprenticed to their former enslaver.[34]

Samuel Coston initially succeeded in taking possession of Leah's children. But Leah knew her constitutional rights and dared to use them. After gaining her legal freedom, she enlisted a team of sympathetic lawyers to help rescue her children.

In the end, it was proven that Samuel Coston had no legal grounds to keep Leah's children. He was forced to return them—a rare victory so notable that the *New York Times* reported on it.[35] For most Black mothers and fathers, however, family separation remained a common outcome in their long struggles against their lifelong oppressors.

Involuntary apprenticeship was prevalent across all former slaveholding states in the South. It emerged alongside other forms of forced labor, such as debt peonage, fixed-term slavery, convict leasing, and the chain gang system. Like these systems, it was shaped by the carceral system, compelling children with incarcerated parents to work under white control.

This was particularly true for children whose mothers were convicted of vagrancy; by law, they could be apprenticed to white "masters" until adulthood. But what about the children of mothers incarcerated for other nonviolent "crimes" or felony convictions?

Although it's not completely clear, evidence suggests that some children lived with their fathers or other relatives while their mothers were incarcerated. Children born to mothers in prison, however, often had fewer opportunities for kinship care. In many cases, the state—or its representatives, such as prison administrators—made decisions regarding their care.

When Mary Morst became pregnant, she never envisioned giving birth in prison. As a first-time mother to twins, she likely celebrated and feared the experience; in 1913, multiple births carried significant risks for infants and mothers. But for abused mothers like Mary, the risks were even greater.

"John Morst was not a nice man, especially when he drank," Mary Morst's great-granddaughter Kimberlea wrote candidly about her great-grandfather. She goes on to explain why Mary ended his life. In her final moments as his wife, Mary cleaned the house and cooked dinner as she always did. She fixed her husband's plate first—a common gesture among Black women in Southern communities to show love, respect, and care for their men. John showed his feelings for Mary too, expressing his "gratitude" by taking her plate of food and feeding it to the dog. Worn down by years of physical and mental abuse, and now pregnant, Mary had enough: she "snapped" and, in a fit of rage, killed her partner.[36]

Mary must have known how bad things could get if a jury found her guilty. Around the time of her trial, Virginia—the state where she lived—had just electrocuted its first female in history: a seventeen-year-old Black girl named Virginia Christian. Mary likely feared that she might be next.

Fortunately, Mary survived. Instead of sending her and her unborn twins to the electric chair, a judge sentenced her to eighteen years in the Virginia State Penitentiary. It was an imperfect end to a marriage that had soured but produced two innocent children.

On January 13, 1913, Mary gave birth to Joseph and Martha. After all she had endured, one can only imagine the emotions she must have felt holding them for the first time. In her day, imprisoned mothers were allowed to cradle their babies with both hands; their wrists were not shackled to hospital beds during labor, as became common since the late twentieth century and only recently outlawed. Mary also had the privilege of raising her children inside the prison, at least for their first few years, in stark contrast to today's policies that separate imprisoned mothers from their newborns within forty-five minutes to forty-eight hours, depending on the state. But when her children turned four, Mary was forced to say good-bye. Under Virginia law, once a child reached this age, they were taken back to the county or city from which the mother came and "disposed of" as the court saw fit.

In a passionate letter, Mary pleaded with the prison superintendent to give her children a good home: "Mr. Wood: Dear Sir I will write and aske you will you pleas grant me the priveledge of given my two children to Emma J. Randolph as I has nothing in here and she has grown children who can take them and rais them and take care of them and I am willing and well satisfied with her having them pleas sir I pledge. Your Humble Servant Mary Moss 11033."[37] Mary advocated for her children's future, hoping Mr. Wood would see value in placing them with a family. He answered by ignoring her request and placing her children in an orphanage.

Mary dreaded losing Martha and Joseph to an involuntary adoption. Though she had no parental rights, she began seeking a pardon with the support of Kate Plecker, a teacher in the prison who took pity on her. In a letter petitioning for Mary's release, Plecker described her love for her children as "pathetic in the extreme," noting how Mary spent whatever little money she had on "a bit of gingham" or "wearing apparel" to ensure her children would have nice clothes when they returned to her. Plecker concluded in her letter: "she has a real mother heart."[38]

Even from behind the walls, Mary did her best to raise, protect, and provide for her children. She cared for them as deeply as any mother—captive or free. Her imprisonment did not diminish the emotional bond she shared with her babies. Just as the auction block could not sever Black mothers' connections to their children, neither could the cell block.

Hope sustained Mary through her prison term, along with dreams of returning to Martha and Joseph. Mercy eventually set her free. In April 1921, a Virginia governor granted her a conditional pardon, marking the end of her bondage and the beginning of a new life. With a few dollars from doing extra work in prison, she traveled to West Virginia to live with her father. She supported them working as a servant for a white family. After his death in 1931, she made the decision to leave the South entirely, joining the Great Migration—a movement that saw an estimated 1.5 million Black Americans escaping racial oppression and pursuing better economic opportunities in the North and the Midwest.

Mary set out for Ohio alone, not because she wanted to but because she did not have her children. At seventeen, Joseph was being held as an "inmate" at the West Virginia State and Industrial School for Colored Boys, and Martha had already married a much older man and had a son.[39]

Being a poor Black teenager in the Depression-era South increased Martha's chances of ending up in a state-run juvenile facility, like Joseph. Perhaps her marriage was a way to break free from a system that had controlled her life since she was in the womb. Having an adult male to provide for her could ensure her future survival and offer a pathway to freedom.

With one child in a juvenile detention center and the other bound in wedlock, Mary continued reshaping her life—marrying a new husband and exploring possibilities in a former free state, perhaps far beyond Jane Crow's inequality. It was an extraordinary outcome, particularly at a time when it was almost impossible for a Black woman to find her way home from prison. For some, the only path home came through severe illness or death.

"To night i am surffring and bleeding as though you was killing hogs," wrote Ella Gamble to Joseph S. Turner, head of the Georgia Prison

Commission on July 31, 1904. "I have been down sick in bed 12 months to day Judge i dont feel like i will be here on earth very long," she explained. The cancer in her bowels, bladder, and womb had reached the final stage, leaving her with no other option but to petition for her freedom.

"Kind sir i write to you and humbly beg you to please send me home," Ella pleaded. "I do not want to die here in prison." Ella still believed she could be cured. Not only did she want to be free, she wanted to live. "Please help me to save my life," she requested of Judge Turner. "For the [L]ord sake Judge i humble beg you to send me home to my brother so he can have me cure."[40]

Ella had served nineteen years, two months, and twenty-one days in the Georgia state prison system—nearly half of her life. She had entered the system in 1884, when she was just twenty years old. And at thirty-nine, she left it barely clinging to life.

Before her conviction, Ella had been working as a domestic servant in a white household—one of the few jobs available to a poor Black woman in the South, where Jane Crow's inequalities shaped everything about her freedom, including employment options. But she still had a decent life, which included a unified family that had survived chattel slavery, a new husband, and a viable pregnancy—Ella had just conceived when her troubles started.

Her day began just like any other, working in the kitchen of Mr. and Mrs. Buchanan. She fed them well, cleaned their kitchen, then prepared to go home. But on this day, Mrs. Buchanan "ordered her to leave." Ella, "having incurred the jealousy" of her mistress, went about her way, leaving the couple's home for her own. It would be her last time serving the Buchanans—or experiencing life as a free individual.[41]

A jury took just two hours to find Ella guilty. Overwhelmed by a mountain of circumstantial evidence and a racially biased judicial system, she faced an unavoidable injustice. Ella would be sentenced to spend the rest of her life in the Georgia state prison system for fatally poisoning Mr. Buchanan—a crime she consistently denied committing.

At the time of her conviction, Ella was three months pregnant. Aware of her condition, the state decided to lease her to Benjamin G. Lockett's brickyard. There she continued in the same occupation she held in the free world, cooking. After giving birth, she was transferred to James English's Chattahoochee brickyard where she remained until she was later sent to his Bolton broom factory.[42]

It was at the broom factory that Ella Gamble met Rose Henderson, Nora Lay, and other women serving life sentences in the state system. She shared their burdens and their faith in God, expressed during Rose's spirit-filled Sunday school services. At one meeting, Ella offered parting words that foreshadowed the future: "If I never see you all no more I hope to see you in heaven."[43]

Ella continued to see the women every day, traveling with them through various stops in Georgia's prison system, including the Camp Heardmont plantation and the Georgia state prison farm. By the time she reached the state farm in 1899, Ella was still capable of providing labor to the state. However, her health was declining without her knowledge, as routine physicals were not offered to incarcerated women then (something still true now). By the time she applied for executive clemency, she had endured nearly twenty years of hard labor, physical and sexual abuse resulting in multiple pregnancies, the death of two babies, and debilitating cancer exacerbated by hard labor and violence against her. The only thing left was her right to live—or die—in freedom, so she advocated for that right, acknowledging that the state would no longer profit from keeping her bound. "I am no service to myself and neither the state," she asserted. "Judge please have mercy on me."[44]

Ella received the mercy she petitioned for and was set free from the state of Georgia on August 10, 1904. She lived her final moments as a free woman, fulfilling the dream of seeing her family again. She had waited nearly two decades to, in her own words, "see there faces once more on earth." But any hopes she might have held for reuniting with her living children remained unspoken in her letters to Judge Turner. She spoke only of her "mother and brother and sister," not her four living children or the husband of her youth.

Assuming all her children were born in the system—and there is a strong possibility that they were—they would have been disposed of according to state laws, if there were any. To date, I have not seen evidence of such laws, likely because during the convict leasing period—when Ella was in her childbearing years—there was no legal precedent for dealing with children born in private labor camps. This helps explain the prevalence of infant death during this period; the historical record is filled with examples of babies being killed violently by prison guards or lost to starvation and illness. It also helps explain the disappearance of children in the system, children whose births were recorded in physicians' reports but who became untraceable beyond those official documents.

For over twenty years, I have been searching for Ella's missing children. The only significant record I have found is a 1900 census of the Georgia state prison farm, which lists Ella as having six children—four living and two deceased. Beyond that, no additional records detail their lives.[45]

Tracing Ella's journey as a mother has proven equally challenging. During her incarceration, she was assigned to five different labor camps. Very few official documents produced by the prison system mention her being a mother, aside from a single reference to the child she carried in her womb the day she was sentenced to life in prison.

Locating the children of imprisoned women today is easier than in the past. They live behind the walls of jails, in prisons, in state-funded group homes, in foster homes, with relatives, or with strangers appointed by the court system as their new parents. Their stories, however, are far harder to trace; without access to confidential case files that document their lived experiences, one cannot fully understand the depth of their suffering or the state's role in it. This is why personal testimonies are so important. They fill a crucial gap in our understanding of a system that is otherwise difficult to grasp.

On November 17, 2021, I had the privilege of speaking at the Peace and Justice Summit on Family Wellness, organized by A New Way of Life Reentry Project in Los Angeles, California. The event brought together state and county officials, attorneys, academics, community organizers, and survivors to discuss existing family separation policies and promote a community vision for child welfare that better supports family reunification. During the event, I provided expert testimony as a historian, offering a historical perspective on the harsh realities faced by victims of Los Angeles County's child welfare system, one of the largest in the nation. I also listened to moving testimonies from mothers, children, and fathers recently affected by the loss of their loved ones.

I can still hear the tremble in grown women's voices as they described their experiences of being little girls raised by the state, moved from one household to another without ever having a real home. They expressed feeling unloved by their foster "parents," who treated them as objects of profit. In the United States, foster parents receive a stipend from the state intended to provide food, shelter, and clothing for children in their care, yet many children are still deprived of these basic needs.

State-sponsored, monetized foster care remains central to America's child "welfare" system. The same is true for financially motivated adoptions. The federal Adoption and Safe Families Act (ASFA) encourages adoptions from the public foster care system by providing financial incentives from the federal government. Under the ASFA-based Adoption Incentive Program (renamed the Adoption and Legal Guardianship Incentive Payments Program in 2014), states receive funds to motivate and reward them for facilitating quick and permanent placements for children in the foster care system. Since its inception, the program has paid out over $1 billion. However, to continue to qualify for these adoption incentive payments, states must adopt more children—and break up more families—than they did the previous year.[46]

In comparison, wild horses and donkeys fare better than America's poorest children. Let me explain: a federal program created by the Bureau of Land Management in 2019—a program that directly mirrors ASFA's AIP program—does not require yearly increases in adoption numbers for animals. This program's sole focus has been to place at-risk animals into "good, loving homes" while reducing the costs of their care by providing adopters a one-thousand-dollar incentive, a benefit that remains even if states do not exceed the previous year's quota. However, the program was shut down in March 2025 by a court order over concerns of cruel and inhumane treatment.[47]

The Adoption and Safe Families Act not only uses required quotas and financial incentives from the Adoption Incentive Program to separate families, it also mandates that states initiate adoptions within a set time frame. One of the most devastating provisions is the 15/22 rule, which requires that states petition to terminate parental rights for any child who has been in foster care for fifteen out of the most recent twenty-two months. What this means is that parents, especially mothers, incarcerated for more than fifteen months risk permanently losing their children unless a family member assumes custody.

The 15/22 rule places Black mothers at a severe disadvantage. They face higher rates of incarceration (and always have), longer sentences, and insufficient resources to pay bail and other fees to secure their freedom. Courts are also more likely to label them as "unfit," neglectful, or absent—racial stereotypes that have been used to justify taking Black women's children for as long as America has existed as a nation. Coupled with the stigma of incarceration, the permanent loss of one's children becomes the *expected* outcome. One of the most enduring consequences of Jane Crow's inequality is the deep-rooted, racially biased assumption that Black women are unworthy as mothers—a bias that has plagued them since chattel slavery.

In some cases, a state may fast-track an adoption, bypassing efforts to reunify the family altogether. Stephanie's story, which appears at the beginning of this chapter, is a prime example. Her baby was adopted more quickly than the fifteen-month rule requires, highlighting the significant value placed on her child by the state. Infants are easier to adopt out. For this reason, there is a motivation to prioritize them for expedited adoptions, as it allows the state to off-load them before they decline in value to prospective adopters.

Children become harder to place as they get older, with the likelihood of adoption decreasing significantly after age nine and even more so for teenagers. To counter this, more money is offered by the federal government to states to adopt these children out; the more difficult it is to place a child, the more financial incentives are offered to states to find them permanent homes. The irony is no extraordinary measures are taken to reunify these children with their parents, nor are monetary benefits offered that might help families raise their own children.

It would be reckless to assume that every Black child in the child "welfare" system is unwanted by their parents or has been abused. This is a racial myth. There are times when parents willingly give up their children or when child welfare appears to be the only solution for rescuing a child from abuse or danger, but poverty often drives the separation of families. These children hold immense value to their biological mothers and fathers, a value that may not be recognized by the state or others evaluating their worth on the ASFA auction block.

While foster parents receive financial benefits to care for children officially declared wards of the state, they are not obligated to love them. The hidden cost of paying strangers to care for other people's children is the suffering these children often endure. Sometimes, it occurs in the form of physical and sexual abuse, and other times, it involves withholding nurture or other basic human needs.

Rather than support parents who love their children but struggle to provide for them financially, the state chooses to pay private individuals to care for them instead. Then when a parent engages in a nonviolent "crime," such as stealing for survival or leaving underage children home alone during work because they cannot afford childcare, they are punished. Every day, desperate acts of love result in incarceration and separation for Black mothers and fathers who sacrifice everything for their children—including their freedom.

It is shocking but true that in the twenty-first century, state-sponsored abduction of children as punishment for poverty and incarceration is as prevalent as it was during the peak of the War on Drugs. The life-changing revelations shared during the Peace and Justice Summit, along with one-on-one conversations with survivors since, confirmed this for me. I have learned that the child "welfare" system, in its current form, is not a benevolent solution to neglect and abandonment, especially if you are a descendant of chattel slavery. It is a system that tears families apart—something I feared as a child but deeply suppressed until authoring this book.

As a child, I lived in greater fear of CPS than I ever did of a home invasion. Family separation was a dreaded consequence of poverty in my community—one that people banded together to prevent. After writing *Searching for Jane Crow*, I now better understand what could have happened to me if I had given the wrong answers to my white teachers' invasive questions about my mother, her work schedule, my "absent" (actually deceased) father, or any battle scars I might have sustained from having too much fun with my friends. In this last example, I am referencing the types of interrogations children from poor Black communities are subjected to when they come to school with scabs, bruises, or injuries from play. There is often a perception of harm and neglect, even when there is no reason for it. My siblings and I never appeared poor; we ate well, were always clean and well-dressed, and spoke perfect English. Now I know why my mother insisted on it.

For my mother, who was an unlicensed social worker, losing a child to the system was a community failure, which is partly why she kept two refrigerators to help feed our community's children when their mothers became addicted to crack cocaine in the 1980s. During this period, the War on Drugs intensified, resulting in the mass incarceration of Black mothers everywhere, including Ypsilanti, Michigan, where I spent most of my childhood. Like Black men, Black women were disproportionately incarcerated for drug-related convictions, which had an especially devastating impact on their families; most of these women were the primary caregivers for their children. While the storm of incarceration and family loss ripped through Black women's households, they endured yet another threat: the media. Television stations, newspapers, politicians, and anyone with a platform and agenda to promote the War on Drugs took an opportunity to publicly denigrate Black mothers, labeling them "crack whores" and their children "crack babies." This public attack on Black women served to reinforce harmful stereotypes, resulting in them being criminalized and deemed "unfit" for motherhood *and* freedom.

Having lived through the crack era, its propaganda and predatory encroachment on impoverished Black communities—I still remember visits from McGruff the Crime Dog to my local elementary school—I recognize how important personal testimonies are in telling this history. More importantly, I understand the value of centering the voices of survivors of the War on Drugs and the mass incarceration it created. Only through their stories can we gain genuine insights into its impact and consequences, including the development of child "welfare" policies such as ASFA and the expansion of what scholar Dorothy Roberts calls the "family policing system."[48]

The ongoing family separation epidemic continues to create significant challenges for Black families, who have fought for centuries to stay united. To illustrate the current impact of this epidemic and the challenges that persist, I will conclude this chapter by sharing several stories of resilience. These stories reveal the power of love, which transcends systems and familial loss.

Myesha Johnson's story begins with her birth into a close-knit family and to a mother who loved her but struggled with addiction. This illness prevented her from caring for Myesha as she would have wished, leading to her losing custody when Myesha was just one year old. It was 1993, just one year before the passage of the Clinton Crime Bill.

Myesha's aunt took over the responsibility of raising her until she reached her teenage years. In high school, Myesha moved in with her sister but eventually entered the custody of the state of California. She explained her sister's difficult decision to place her in the system, a choice she did not want to make but felt was necessary.

Families often make tremendous sacrifices to stay together, pooling whatever resources they have to care for their loved ones—until they can no longer manage. Financial burdens can push caregivers to their limits, sometimes forcing them to place their relatives under state control as the only way to secure the financial support they need. Unless kinship caregivers become formally licensed as foster parents, they are in most cases ineligible to receive payments from the state. In other words, unless a family member agrees to place a child in the system—and accepts the risk of having them removed from their home at any moment—they cannot receive financial support to care for them.

"Being put in the system at that age, I was . . . very scared," Myesha remembered. "I wasn't used to living with strangers." She recalled her difficulty adjusting to being part of the system: "I felt like I was a piece of property."[49]

Her social worker—whom she compared to an overseer—tracked her every move. She showed up at the foster homes where Myesha lived and even followed her to school. While most children bear the occasional embarrassment of a parent showing up unexpectedly, Myesha endured the shame of her worker appearing at school *every day*. "Your worker's here" served as a dreaded public announcement of her status as state property. But the daily check-ins were required by law, and she had to endure them. "You can't make money if you don't have the product in place," Myesha told me, explaining the rationale for these routine visits. The worker had a duty to secure the state's property. It was the equivalent of an overseer taking inventory of an enslaver's human workforce, or a prison guard performing a random count to ensure everyone is present. Myesha had no choice but to show up. If she ran away, she could face carceral consequences, which included being confined to a state-run group home, a form of home detention for youth. "If you run away from a home, you're called AWOL [absent without leave] . . . Once they find you, there's consequences for you," she explained.

For several years, Myesha endured this new reality. Then, around her eighteenth birthday, her social worker showed up at the foster home where she lived and presented her with emancipation papers. "From that day forward, you're free," Myesha recalled. But freedom came with challenges she did not expect. She was sent out into the world with nothing, as the state did not offer any resources to support her transition to freedom. "It goes back to slavery. You are only of use for so long and when they're done with you you're done," she concluded of her experience. As an emancipated person, Myesha had to face many of the same challenges that returning citizens from prison do—like her mother, who fortunately also regained her freedom.

But freedom held a joyful side for Myesha and her mother. The two solidified their bond before Myesha's mother passed away. Myesha had lost a lot of years with her mother, but they made lasting memories, among them watching her mother "wake up every morning and send all of our family members a scripture." Myesha's mother left behind a legacy of love within her family, despite enduring years of unjust punishment for a condition she needed support to control.

Kyndia Riley also clung to memories of her parents after losing them both to life sentences. Like Myesha's mother, they had become victims of the War on Drugs, entering prison in 1999 when Kyndia was just a year old. With her parents gone, she ran the risk of being abducted into the child "welfare" system and involuntarily adopted. But her grandparents claimed her before the state could take her, raising her and her sister despite significant financial hardship.

"I wasn't able to have all the things other kids had," Kyndia remembered of her childhood in Baltimore, Maryland. But she had the love of her family, which included her parents. Although she did not get to see them frequently, they built a strong connection through letters, occasional phone calls, emails, pictures, homemade gifts, and in-person visits at the prison. When Kyndia's grandparents could scrape up the money, they would drive her and her sister "eleven hours for a six-hour visit," turning the family van into a makeshift hotel room. Their financial struggles cost them time with their incarcerated loved ones; Kyndia saw her father fewer than five times in twenty-three years and went a full ten years without seeing her mother "because we just didn't have the money anymore."[50]

Kyndia's parents did the best they could to help raise her from behind bars. They saved pennies they earned in prison for an entire month just to buy one birthday card. Her mother would ask her what she wanted for her birthday a year in advance, carefully budgeting to buy construction paper to make paper roses or other crafts to show her love. "She would crochet me hats or little teddie bears," Kyndia remembered. "She made me a pop-up Hello Kitty [and a large] ocean horizon painting," she fondly recalled, assigning deep sentimental value to the letters she received. "Being able to share memories through paper, and they never get erased . . . means a lot," she concluded. Most of her parents' letters "were about what they hoped to do, or what they were excited to do, what they planned to do when they came home."

Both of Kyndia's parents eventually made it home, her mother on January 31, 2019, and her father in June 2022. They celebrated their reunion, carefully navigating the challenges families face trying to rebuild broken connections. Establishing bonds beyond the walls can be one of the most difficult parts of the readjustment process after someone returns home. When individuals are incarcerated, they enter a time capsule, and when they are released, they must adapt to the world they left behind—including physical connection. "I had never seen my parent's feet before . . . I had never seen their ankles . . . They had always been in suits," Kyndia explained, describing the many firsts she experienced with her parents. These included shopping together, taking car rides, listening to music, and eating meals together—beyond the bags of Cheetos or other "good snacks" from the prison vending machine during visits.

Since her parents returned home, Kyndia has shared significant milestones with them. However, there are a few life-defining moments that she will never experience with her parents, including the funerals of her grandparents and sister. Unfortunately, she lost the rest of her family while her parents were incarcerated. And she will always carry the memory of graduating from the University of Virginia without her parents there to cheer her on.

The stories of Myesha and Kyndia reflect the experiences of countless children who have either been caught up in the child "welfare" system or narrowly escaped it during their parents' incarceration. They also reflect the current struggles parents face in maintaining, rediscovering, or restoring broken family bonds due to imprisonment, illness in the form of addiction, poverty, or all three, which is often the case for Black families.

The end of chattel slavery did not mark the end of family separation. This epidemic has persisted for centuries and has proven as destructive to Black families in the modern era as it was in the past. While some states, including Texas, have recently passed legislation to enable parents to petition for the restoration of their parental rights when a child has not been successfully adopted, there is still no concerted effort or investment in keeping families together. And for parents, especially Black mothers, a history of incarceration makes matters worse, often resulting in the loss of their children forever or an endless struggle to protect or regain their parental rights.

Today, family reunification remains one of the biggest challenges facing Black mothers reentering society. After returning home from jail or prison, they confront Jane Crow's mountain of racial inequalities, including barriers to reunification, extensive restrictions on their freedoms, and various fees and costs that hinder their ability to maintain connections with their children. Part of confronting this mountain of racial inequalities also means fighting to stay free. The systems of parole and probation have historically made it more difficult for Black women to unchain themselves from the criminal legal system. These systems monitor every aspect of their movements toward freedom, doing everything possible to return them to a state of confinement, reminiscent of the days of chattel slavery.

CHAPTER 6

TRACKING FREEDOM

"Dear Gentlemen: I am writing you in reference to myself. . . . I went to the office Monday morning to report to you Gentlemen, but on my arrival I did not find either one of you there and for fear I would be locked up I came to Macon and reported to Captain Etheredge and asked him to report to you all for me. I did not intend to run away at all whatever . . . and I hope you wont consider me a runaway as I did not intend to do same."

—MATTIE LEE REID, in a letter to
the prison commissioners of Georgia.[1]

On Thanksgiving Day, November 23, 1922, after nearly eight years in prison, Mattie had finally been granted parole by the state's governor. She had a lot to be thankful for as she could finally return to a free life, or so she thought. Yet her "freedom" came with conditions. Being on parole meant she would be allowed to serve the remainder of her sentence outside of prison, but it also meant that she would have to work as a domestic in a white household.

The state hired out Mattie to Mrs. L. S. Archer of Atlanta, Georgia. The arrangement, though exploitative, brought her one step closer to freedom. It gave her an opportunity to live in a nice home on Peachtree

Street, as opposed to the barracks of the state prison farm, and a level of mobility she lacked at the farm.

Even on her grocery runs for Mrs. Archer, Mattie enjoyed a sense of liberty she had not experienced since becoming state property. However, Mrs. Archer soon reminded her of her lack of rights, deciding to relocate to another part of the city and take Mattie with her. But Mattie thwarted Mrs. Archer's plans and moved to Macon, Georgia.

"She would often cry and say she did not want to move—and would not know the way back to the city," Mrs. Archer wrote to the prison commission following Mattie's disappearance. "I can truthfully say, she was treated as a member of the family," she continued, expressing regrets over "getting this woman paroled." But Mattie had served her and her family well, upholding her end of an unfair agreement before choosing to break it.[2]

Anger got the best of Mrs. Archer. She felt cheated by Mattie, who she believed owed her for the room, board, clothes, and money she "gave" her. Mrs. Archer would not rest until Mattie was back in chains: "I think she has grossly violated her parole and in justice to other paroled prisoners I think she should be returned to the state farm to complete her sentence."

Mattie tried to explain her actions in her letter: "I got dissatisfied with Mrs. Archie and I don't want to stay with her." Leaving was not an option she had the legal authority to exercise, but Mattie left anyway, knowing her actions placed her in danger of being violated and potentially returned to prison. She knew not having a job would automatically result in re-incarceration, so she quickly contacted Captain Etheredge, a former sheriff, who hired her out to a white woman in Macon.

"I am well satisfied here and hope you gentlemen will let me remain here as I want to make my paroled time according to the law," Mattie wrote to the commissioners. Mrs. E. A. Barker, her new employer, wrote a letter too: "I want to ask you Gentlemen (if it be possible) let me have this woman."[3]

Mattie's only goal was to fulfill the conditions of her parole and get completely free from the system. However, she found herself trapped in an endless cycle of bondage. As a person on domestic parole, she had to answer to two "masters"—her enslaver, the state of Georgia, and the person who hired her out from the state. She had no rights of her own, just a long list of rules and punishments. For quitting her job and moving out of Mrs. Archer's house without permission, the prison commissioners chose to violate Mattie. "Under the law it is our duty to have paroled prisoners who escape arrested and this is your authority to arrest Mattie Lee Reid," they wrote to the sheriff of Bibb County. "This woman escaped from Mrs. Archer of Atlanta. . . . You will please arrest her and turn her over to Mr. D. P. Jones to be returned to the State Farm," they instructed.[4]

In America today, the systems of parole and probation—collectively known as community supervision—still serve as a key barrier to freedom for Black women. Like Mattie, many remain trapped in a cycle of reincarceration for violating the terms of their freedom. Missing an appointment with a parole or probation officer, breaking curfew, associating with family members who have criminal convictions, being unable to maintain stable employment, being unhoused, and missing a payment for supervision fees (people are required to pay monthly fees for their appointments with parole and probation officers) are just a few of the countless infractions that could send someone back to prison or jail. Because they are still under the supervision of the criminal legal system, they are not fully free. Their captivity extends beyond the bars, which for Black women has historically meant trading one "Big House" for another.

The system of parole is particularly relevant to the history of Black women and mass incarceration, as it has long served to perpetuate slavery. It involves enduring what I call "supervised freedom," which encompasses historical systems of community supervision, such as guardianship and domestic parole, and contemporary parole practices.

For the millions of Black women who have experienced supervised freedom, this has meant constantly fighting to maintain their liberty before the courts and authorities assigned to oversee their freedom; living under boundaries placed on their freedom, enforced by legislation designed to control their lives outside of prison; and having their freedom revoked if they violate their conditional liberty by committing a crime.

This chapter examines the history of parole for Black women, beginning in the early nineteenth century before the system was formally established, through its inception in the early twentieth century, and to the present. It examines how Jane Crow's injustices, primarily in the form of supervised freedom, have shaped their historical experiences, setting a precedent for the conditional freedom they endure today. From behind the walls of private white households, governors' and presidents' mansions, and parole offices, the story of Black women's struggle for freedom is told.

Supervised freedom has existed for Black women for as long as mass incarceration. Beginning in the early nineteenth century, when free Black individuals were entering jails at an alarming rate, Southern states passed laws restricting their liberty. Among these laws was a system known as guardianship, which enforced the supervision of their freedom.

The guardianship system required free Black women and men to be supervised by a white individual who could vouch for their character and take responsibility for them. Having a court-approved guardian was a legal requirement in states such as North Carolina, South Carolina, Georgia, and Florida. It was also a necessity: in many cases, for a free person to conduct business and legal affairs, they had to secure a white guardian's permission.

Without a white guardian, free Black people could not legally exercise liberties granted to white individuals, including the ability to own property, administer a will, sign a contract, or travel. Under the Georgia Guardianship Statute of 1808, free people were legally required to secure approval from their guardians before leaving town. Guardians also had the power to enforce curfews and collect cash payments in the form of supervision fees.[5]

Guardianship relationships, though intended to tightly control free Black individuals, sometimes resulted in unanticipated benefits. According to historian Janice Sumler-Edmond, "Guardians sometimes assisted their black wards in establishing and furthering business interests, securing property, or maintaining credit."[6] But the system itself reinforced white authority, using incarceration and enslavement to punish those who resisted it. Failing to secure a guardian could result in a person being arrested as a "fugitive," their freedom revoked through sale into chattel slavery.

Eliza Saturday Curtis could not afford the risk of being sentenced to slavery. She had two children, William and Frank, and property to protect. So, she did the only thing she could: in 1842, she petitioned the court in Jefferson County, Georgia, to request its approval to appoint Bryant Wasden as her legal guardian.[7]

The freedom of Nancy Coleman and her four children, Mary, Thomas, Baker, and Jincy, became threatened when their guardian, Thomas Barnes, died. To keep her family together, in 1836, she secured a new guardian, Peter Scott. Patsey King, a single woman living in Troup County, Georgia, also took steps to protect her freedom. In 1853, she secured William H. Kistler as her guardian, hoping it would shield her from further exposure to "all the pains and penalties, enacted against free persons of Color, having no Guardian in this State."[8]

Freedom supervision was one of the most demeaning aspects of Jane Crow's injustice. It imposed white authority over Black women under the guise of protection, highlighting the fact that Black women—who lacked true safety—were considered worthy of it only when it placed them under white control. Nevertheless, to ensure their own survival, they obeyed the law, opting for second-class freedom rather than no freedom at all.

"While the freedmen must and will be protected in their rights," stated Orlando Brown, Virginia's assistant commissioner of the Freedmen's Bureau, "they must be required to meet these first and most essential conditions of a state of freedom, a visible means of support, and a fidelity to contracts."[9] His comments revealed the agency's hidden approach to uplifting freed people, who from 1865 to 1872 relied on its assistance—hard labor.

Laboring for white landowners became a condition of freedom that federal agents widely enforced. To maintain good standing with the agency, Black women and men had to secure employment, which usually meant returning to the fields. While the bureau, best known for providing relief to Black people, supported their transition to freedom, the agency also played a role in overseeing it.

As freedom supervisors, they imposed rules and conditions forcing Black people to labor—even if it meant contracting themselves to former slaveholders. As second-class free people, they were not allowed to reject "honest" employment or to take a rest from slavery's toil. Doing so could result in the violation of one's freedom.

Forasmuch as the Freedmen's Bureau did to ensure fair treatment of freed people, it penalized Black individuals, particularly Black women, for exercising their right not to work. Historian Mary Farmer-Kaiser shows that many Black women were prosecuted in the courts of the Freedmen's Bureau for this freedom violation. Although these courts were meant to secure justice for newly freed individuals against the abuses of their Southern white neighbors, they often upheld the same injustices against Black women that they aimed to prevent.

One of the first steps that Black families took to assert their independence was to withdraw women's labor from the fields. In response, the bureau attempted to force freedwomen to work by insisting that their husbands sign contracts that would require the entire family to labor on the land. However, some Black women chose not to comply.

When contracts failed to coerce Black women back into the cotton fields, Freedmen's Bureau officials turned to the criminal legal system to enforce vagrancy laws against them. To be clear, the bureau declared that unemployed freedwomen, except in exceptional cases, should be prosecuted as vagrants. Although not the sole force behind the mass jailing of Black women after Emancipation, the Freedmen's Bureau played a role in escalating imprisonment rates for Black women who dared to "play the lady."[10]

As discussed in previous chapters, vagrancy was a "crime" often linked to poverty. However, it is essential to recognize Black women labeled as vagrants because they refused to work, including mothers and wives who prioritized caring for their families over laboring in the fields or serving in white households. By choosing family devotion, Black women had their freedom taken away. The inequality created by Jane Crow punished Black women for what was often valued in white households—being a stay-at-home mother and wife.

Choosing to retire from the fields without white permission was a crime and freedom violation. Bureau agents punished Black women by reporting them to authorities. Their actions set a precedent for how Black women's freedom would be supervised in the twentieth century, a period when the system of parole became the primary enforcer of supervised freedom.

Dr. James P. Westmoreland, a respected surgeon in Houston, Texas, provided a comfortable life for his wife, Grace. He employed Black servants to work for her while he helped save lives, including a Black man named George Washington. He also hired out Anna Bell Johnson from the Texas state prison system.

Before being sentenced to prison and later paroled to Dr. Westmoreland, Anna lived in a modest home of her own in Queen City, Texas. She had earned her living by cooking for a white family and even had a little money to her name, as evidenced by a gold tooth she proudly wore. However, something went wrong, leading her to become entangled in the criminal legal system.

On October 17, 1924, Anna was convicted of burglary and sentenced to ten years' labor at the Goree State Prison Farm for women.[11] Established in 1911, the one-thousand-acre plantation was named for Thomas Jewett Goree, a former Confederate soldier and prison superintendent, not the island off the coast of Senegal, West Africa, as some might think.[12]

The women who lived and labored there were mostly of African descent, captive to the Texas prison system.

Goree, like other state prison farms, served to bring incarcerated women under state control rather than in the hands of private landowners. Before 1911, women prisoners were leased to privately owned plantations in Texas. Their transfer to Goree coincided with Progressive era calls to end convict leasing in the state following reports of abuse.

At Goree, women prisoners were segregated by race according to state law. Jane Crow divided Black and white women in their living quarters, social worlds, and labor. It ensured separation in every aspect of life, including where they slept, ate, and even sat at the prison rodeo. Segregation was especially pronounced in their labor assignments: white women worked inside the prison garment factory with Hispanic women, while Black women labored in the fields. Anna worked in the kitchen.

Despite escaping from Goree six months into her sentence, Anna made parole. As states implemented their first parole laws at the turn of the twentieth century, Texas followed suit. In 1905, the Texas legislature passed its initial law giving the Board of Pardon Advisors and the Board of Prison Commissioners authority to grant parole. With the governor's approval, they could recommend any person who had served two years or 25 percent of their sentence and proved to be in "good standing."[13] By November 1, 1926, when Anna's case was heard, these laws had evolved even further: the governor had held sole power to grant parole since in 1913.

Anna was not a model prisoner. Yet this did not stop Governor Miriam A. Ferguson, the first female governor of Texas, from approving her parole. She might have taken pity on Anna—or not. Anna was a skilled cook, making her easy to hire out under the state's domestic parole system. Prison labor was cheap and desirable for those looking to exploit house servants. Dr. Westmoreland could pay Anna what he wanted, if he wanted to pay her anything at all. And for the state, freeing Anna's bed at Goree made room for another Black woman.

Anna packed up her life's belongings and headed to Houston to finish out her sentence. She arrived at the Westmoreland house in a quiet, middle-class suburb, much different from the working-class neighborhood she left in Queen City, or the plantation at Goree. It had all the comforts of a desirable home, but it was not hers. She longed to live freely again.

On December 18, 1926, Anna quit, leaving Dr. Westmoreland, his wife, and the state of Texas to look for her. The state issued an all-points bulletin, offering a "$25 Dollars Reward Delivered to Transfer Agent at Any Jail in the United States." Her state identification number, mug shot, fingerprints, physical scars, gold tooth, skull size, shoe size, weight, age, height, names and addresses of family members, and other private details were displayed on an escape record card. This information was circulated to authorities along with her designation as a "PAROLE VIOLATOR."[14]

While the state and her freedom supervisors agonized over her whereabouts, Anna enjoyed her freedom. It was Christmastime, and even for a poor Black woman on the run, the holiday season might have meant something special. It may have been the reason she fled in the first place. Maybe she wanted to be at home with her father, Jim, and Eugene, Spencer, and Lulu, her siblings in Texarkana, Arkansas, instead of at the Westmorelands' place. The thought of preparing a feast for a free family might have been more than she could bear.

Although is unclear how or when Anna was recaptured, the authorities eventually caught up with her. Evidence suggests that she served the entire length of her court-ordered sentence. Whether she completed it in the kitchen at Goree or in a white household, her journey through the Texas state prison system ended on October 17, 1934.[15] Anna returned to her life with no job, no money, and only the clothes on her back, but she had her freedom and the ability to supervise it on her terms.

Title 45, Section 92, of the 1940 Alabama Code reads as follows: "It shall be unlawful to hire or lease for any purpose any convict, state or county." However, state prison director Frank Boswell felt differently, asserting that "every warden has a right to a convict." This served as his defense in

1949 when he was interrogated by a legislative committee investigating Alabama prison conditions.[16]

The practice of hiring prisoners out to white households was legal in Alabama in the 1940s as a condition of parole. But Boswell, Governor James Elisha Folsom, and other prison officials operated an unofficial system of domestic labor, sending Black prisoners who were not on parole to work as servants in the homes of state officials.

Governor Folsom, along with his sister, Ruby Ellis, legal advisor Kenneth Griffith, staff member Mary Hogan, and brother-in-law S. Fleetwood Carnley, illegally hired out Black women prisoners from the Julia Tutwiler Prison for Women to work as servants in their homes. They were joined by Boswell's secretary, Frances Jones, Draper Prison warden Burr Reeves, former Kilby Prison warden and Pardons and Parole Board member Hamp Draper, and the Tutwiler Prison superintendent, Mrs. W. A. Austin.[17]

Established in 1942 as Alabama's first women's prison, Tutwiler played a significant role in providing forced labor. Building a women's prison in the Deep South, naming it after a white female social reformer, and assigning it a rehabilitation mission did not make it any less a place for punishment and profit than a prison named for a former Confederate. Though Tutwiler's stated mission of reform did not encompass involuntary labor, prison officials made sure it occurred anyway. Even the presence of a small number of white women prisoners was not enough to overshadow the legacy of slavery that shaped the experiences of Black women confined in Alabama's prison system.[18]

What happened at Tutwiler in the 1940s was a continuation of exploitative practices Black women had long endured in Alabama's prison system, beginning in the convict leasing era. Between 1869 and 1888, they cooked, cleaned, and sewed for male prisoners at mining camps and farms—and also worked as house servants for male wardens.[19]

From the start, forced labor defined the experiences of Black women incarcerated in Alabama. But it took on new meaning with the introduction of unauthorized parole. Being unofficially held in domestic slavery meant they could not formally apply for parole. It meant being doubly imprisoned—exploited both by the prison system and by the households of those who ran it. It also meant lacking any protection against the arbitrary extension of their sentences based on the needs or demands of their captors.

Illegal domestic slavery bore a close resemblance to debt peonage. It involved kidnapping, coercion, and theft—perpetrators stole Black women and their labor from the state. In other words, they embezzled state property for their personal gain.

Although state officials primarily engaged in this practice, lower-ranking prison employees also unlawfully accessed Black house servants. At least they had to pay for their services. "NOT ALL WHO HAVE NEGRO WOMEN CONVICTS as servants fare as well as the political favorites," Hugh W. Sparrow of the *Birmingham News* reported in his 1948 exposé of the Alabama prison system. An investigation revealed that prison guards paid twelve dollars a month to hire Black women from Tutwiler while "politically influential individuals" paid nothing. "At least one guard has saved receipts for the last 12 or 14 months which prove that the *state* [italics mine] has leased and charged for the leasing of convicts," Sparrow discovered. These payments were made directly to the Department of Corrections and Institutions.[20]

When Dr. J. F. Sewell, a physician in the prison system, fell behind on his payments for the "two negro females" he hired, he received a letter reminding him of his debt. H. C. Flowers, chief of the Division of Prison Welfare, wrote: "In checking the remittances against rosters, we find that you paid only $10.00 for the month of January, and we will have to ask that you contribute an equal amount that every person is now contributing per person." Flowers continued, "If you feel that you cannot pay $20.00 for the two, please turn one of your cooks in, in order that she may be sent out for other placements, as we do not have enough trained, qualified prisoners to meet the demands of the Department's employees."[21]

Bessie Mae Dunford, Lola Mae Scott, Ruth Williams, Mary Lee Brown, Sarah Pugh, Anna Horton, Erma Dee Roberson, Lonzie Lee

Williams, and Clara Coats were among the "qualified" Black women trafficked through Tutwiler in the 1940s, a period when majority of Black women in the South worked as domestic servants. So were Polly Thompson, Grace Lee Norris, Lena Shaw, Viola Potts, Trudie Mae Davis, Elois Boyd, Lucendia Allison, Lizzie Stewart, and Annie Mae Charles.[22] Although wartime production during World War II opened up employment opportunities for all women, Black women in the South still faced Jane Crow's inequality through labor discrimination; as late as 1960, 90 percent of Southern Black women continued to work as domestics.[23] Meanwhile, the region's expanding defense industry created new opportunities for white women, who left traditional roles for jobs in industries such as shipbuilding and aviation. While they contributed the war effort, Black women took care of their children.

It is worth asking how wartime demands and increasing employment opportunities for white mothers impacted the system of domestic parole. Were more Black women paroled into domestic service—both legally and illegally— than would have been the case otherwise? If so, how did the end of World War II and the beginning of the Civil Rights Movement in the 1950s further shape this practice?

Did Black women's resistance to racial segregation, violence, voting disenfranchisement, and other forms of oppression—and the incarceration that resulted from it—grow the population of paroled Black servants? Did employers increasingly hire them to secure a more controllable, exploitable labor force? How did Black women respond? Did they find ways to balance their supervised freedom with their desire to participate in the freedom movement? Did they protest? Or did they secretly donate their earnings instead, if they received any, to invest in the cause, hoping that, upon exiting prison, they might reenter a more just society?

Domestic parole persisted for most of the twentieth century. While it was most prevalent in the Deep South, where the largest number of incarcerated Black women resided, it also occurred throughout the entire United States. As historians Cheryl D. Hicks and Sarah Haley show in their work, paroled Black women worked in white households as far away as New York and the nation's capital, including one who served time in the White House.[24]

Jimmy Carter is best known as the thirty-ninth president of the United States (1977–1981). Less known about him is that, at the time of his presidency, he served as a parole officer for an incarcerated Black woman named Mary Prince.[25] Carter believed in Mary's innocence, and so did his wife. In fact, it was Rosalynn's idea to bring Mary into the family's home to serve out her sentence.

The rest of the story resembles a Cinderella fairy tale: Rosalynn and President Carter rescue an impoverished Black woman from Georgia's cruel criminal legal system, ultimately taking her to work in the White House. But the twist in this otherwise enchanted story is that Mary was legally considered a slave.

Mary was convicted of murder in April 1970, at a time when 70 percent of the nation's female prison population was Black.[26] As a working-class Black woman in the South, she could not afford legal representation and was assigned a court-appointed attorney whom she met twice for ten or fifteen minutes. "In court, I was under the impression I was pleading guilty to involuntary manslaughter but it turned out to be murder," she told a reporter for *People* magazine. "The whole time in court took less than an hour, and I was sentenced right there to life in prison."[27]

Mary Prince was taken to a women's prison in Hardwick, Georgia, where she expected to spend the rest of her life. But her fate changed in December 1970 when prison officials selected her for an interview at the mansion of then governor Jimmy Carter. Mary had been participating in a prison trustee program that allowed prisoners to work at the governor's mansion, similar to the program former president Bill Clinton later used for incarcerated workers at his Arkansas mansion during his tenure as governor (1979–1981).

In her 1996 book *It Takes a Village*, Hillary Rodham Clinton vividly recalled her mixed feelings about "encountering a convicted murderer in the kitchen every morning." "I was apprehensive, but I agreed to abide by tradition," she wrote.[28] This tradition relied on incarcerated labor to keep down costs and included violating the help, Clinton remembered: "We enforced rules strictly and sent back to prison any inmate who broke a rule."[29]

But the Carters welcomed Mary Prince into their home without hesitation, despite her murder conviction. They entrusted her with their three-year-old daughter, Amy, who immediately took to her new nanny. "She liked me to sing 'Swing Low, Sweet Chariot' to her every night," Mary remembered.[30] A song once sung by escaped enslaved people on their journey to freedom was transformed into a lullaby for Amy. Perhaps singing it gave Mary hope for a future beyond her own enslavement.

When Carter's term as governor ended in January 1975, so did Mary's fairy tale. She was sent back to prison. But Rosalynn continued to visit her at the Fulton County Jail and Atlanta Work Release Center where she worked as a cook. When Carter was inaugurated as president in January 1976, she received special permission to travel to Washington, DC, for his inauguration. She slept in the White House and even attended an inaugural ball—the women at the prison sewed a velvet gown for her to wear. Then came the moment that changed her life. "Mrs. Carter said, 'How would you like to work in this big old place?" Mary remembered. Not long after, she was paroled to the White House.

Amy had grown bigger by this time and was enrolled in school. Mary went from being a full-time caregiver, to cleaning the executive mansion. It is how the Carters justified her $6,004 per year salary and third-floor apartment to an angry public who resented the use of taxpayer dollars to support a person with a felony conviction. But Mary earned her keep; whatever extras she received, she deserved.

Having access to gourmet food was little compensation for the meals Mary missed with her sons, who lived in an apartment with her sister while she served the First Family. Being the highest-paid domestic on parole in America was a modest reward for working all day, then taking a taxi to Suitland, Maryland, to see about her boys in the evening. After helping with homework and making sure their school clothes were ready for the next day, Mary would take a taxi back to the White House before daybreak.[31] Amy woke up at 7:30 a.m.

Mary chose not to move her sons into the White House. She did not want her family "under their roof." "That was *my* job," she insisted. She sacrificed to protect her children, paying for their own home, drawing a boundary between her private life and her public duties.[32] Amid the pervasive media portrayal of "welfare queens," the escalating War on Drugs, threatening images of gun-carrying Black power activists, and other racially charged propaganda, Mary's story emerged, capturing public attention and making her famous. Meanwhile, thousands of Black women imprisoned due to the Drug War suffered largely out of the spotlight.

Geneva Cooley lived in obscurity behind the walls of Julia Tutwiler Prison for Women in Wetumpka, Alabama, until a chance meeting with Susan Burton in 2018 changed her life. Moved by her story—sentenced to 999 years, 99 months, and 99 days for riding on a train with a sock full of heroin—Susan made calls that led to a national campaign to free her. Like Mary Prince, Geneva gained national attention. After seventeen years in one of America's worst prisons, she reclaimed her freedom—though she has been on parole since her release in 2019.

I remember the first time I met Geneva in 2022 and learned the details of her story: arrested for possessing drugs she intended to use for her illness; held in Alabama's Jefferson County Jail for four years awaiting trial; sentenced during an election year by a tough-on-crime governor seeking reelection; sentenced to life in prison without parole; and confined in Tutwiler Prison for Women—the same prison where countless Black women were forced into domestic service.

The fact that Geneva had been sentenced to over one thousand years in prison for a nonviolent drug conviction left me in shock. How could carrying a small bag of heroin from New York to Alabama be treated as high-level drug trafficking? I was equally stunned by the fees she had to pay to maintain her freedom.

When Geneva left prison in 2019, she received a $450,000 bill from the state of Alabama. This bill, mostly court fees, was later reduced to $50,000 after she went to court to reduce her sentence to life in prison. Geneva is still paying these fees today. Most months, she sends twenty-five dollars, and other months she sends one hundred dollars. Like most people on parole, Geneva must closely budget her limited resources. As she nears eighty, she is growing less optimistic about her ability to pay off the cost of her freedom in her lifetime.

Today, approximately 3.7 million people in the United States are under fee-based freedom supervision. Like Geneva, they are pinching pennies to pay their supervision fees, which range from ten to sixty-five dollars a month, as well as charges for electronic monitoring for in-home confinement, court fees, and restitution.

Supervision fees generate millions of dollars for state and local governments and private companies each year. While exact totals are hard to calculate, the numbers are estimated in the millions for each state. A 2014 Human Rights Watch report found that private probation companies in Georgia alone collected about $39 million in a single year.[33] In 1990, during the peak of the War on Drugs, Texas probation departments collected approximately $57 million. While these figures have slightly decreased over time, along with the supervised population, Americans still likely pay at least one billion dollars in freedom fees per year.

Unfortunately, the racial disparities across the punishment industry also exist for parole and probation. This is not surprising given the history from which freedom supervision emerged—slavery. Of the 3.7 million people under freedom supervision today, over 30 percent are Black. Although Black individuals make up only 14 percent of the nation's population, they account for about 38 percent of those on parole and 30 percent of those on probation. According to the Equal Justice

Initiative, "Black people are 50 to 100 percent more likely to be charged with parole violations."[34]

Before meeting Geneva Cooley, I had never considered quantifying the cost of freedom. I did not fully understand that people on parole are not truly free. They must carry a travel pass approved by their parole officer before leaving the state. They must pay supervision fees to maintain their conditional liberty or face being returned to state-sanctioned slavery. In states such as Alabama, where Geneva's parole is still active, individuals cannot get off parole until all their court fees are paid. And when they die, the state can collect the remaining debt by seizing any assets. For a low-income individual, this may be everything they own.

Geneva's story reinforces the fact that mass incarceration perpetuates slavery through parole. It closely resembles what historians call "quasi-freedom," which describes the condition of enslaved people who experienced a degree of independence while still legally tied to slavery. This concept highlights the complex reality faced by those who were not fully free but had some autonomy in their daily lives. The only difference today is that paroled—"quasi-free"—people do not receive freedom papers when they are manumitted. Getting *off* paper is what establishes an incarcerated person's legal freedom.

Living on parole today is like living as a free Black person under chattel slavery or as a freed person after Emancipation. It means a vulnerable, uncertain freedom, a freedom that can be undone with the breaking of a single rule, the stroke of a freedom supervisor's pen, or the swing of a judge's gavel. And it is a freedom that can be held ransom through unpaid fees and other costs that keep a person perpetually in bondage.

Still, there is light. Joy and brightness fill Geneva's soul each day she gets to spend with her son and grandchildren in New York, where she currently resides. She breathes fresh air, eats free-world food, selects her own clothing, travels (with a pass), sleeps in a safe, warm bed, and enjoys her golden years. She is still "on paper," the supervisor of her second-class freedom, but she is home—and halfway free.

Geneva is joined by millions of Americans enjoying being home from incarceration. Yet this pleasure is tested by constant threats to their freedom—a job loss, a late bus, missed appointment, or a simple mistake could ruin everything. The histories presented in this chapter demonstrate that this has always been the case: supervised freedom has never led to true liberty. It is merely an extension of mass incarceration and the slavery that created it.[35]

EPILOGUE

SOLUTIONS FOR FREEDOM

When I started writing *Searching for Jane Crow* in 2018, I believed that reforming the criminal legal system was both possible and necessary. However, the process of researching, writing, and reflecting on this book has proven transformative, and today, when people ask me about reforming the system, it feels akin to asking me how to make slavery better.

It has become clear to me that reform does not lead to freedom. It is merely a way to prolong mass incarceration and the slavery that produced it. In other words, reform is what opened the door to all-female convict lease camps run by former enslavers. It is what inspired the creation of chain gangs, state-owned prison farms, women's prisons named for Confederate soldiers, and domestic parole. It is what private prison corporations owe for their existence, and what many private companies rely on for their earnings. And it is the reason why the Adoption and Safe Families Act auction block was built, and why countless mothers and fathers are weeping over the loss of their children as I write this epilogue.

The US punishment industry is massive and unprecedented. It is our modern-day Goliath; a tall, menacing force that threatens the lives of every person that crosses its path. Even so, its large size makes it an easy target. It can be brought down. But who, besides the people that are terrorized by it, will be courageous enough to confront it?

Until Goliath falls, and the people are set free, we must chart our own paths to freedom. It is what enslaved people did hundreds of years ago and what survivors of state-sanctioned slavery are doing today. Many of the solutions I offer here are exemplified by Black women leading the fight for freedom and justice. Who better to seek freedom solutions from than those who have survived being enslaved through the carceral system?

The most obvious solution for freedom is abolishing mass incarceration and investing in people instead. It is seeing value in people, not monetary worth. It is understanding that freedom is a birthright and not a racial privilege. It is caring for people and demonstrating that through concrete actions, as opposed to caging them for their wrongs.

One of the most profound lessons I have learned in my journey writing *Searching for Jane Crow* is that we live in a nation that criminalizes trauma. When an individual experiences physical and sexual violence, mental abuse, poverty, chronic hunger, or the psychological stress of being mass surveilled by police, incarcerated, or separated from loved ones, it can leave them in a deep state of distress. Some turn to drugs to cope. Others engage in behaviors mislabeled as crime, such as stealing to eat, or squatting in an abandoned building or on a park bench after addiction has stripped them of everything, including a place to call home.

For some, this trauma results in acts of violence, particularly self-defense among women. The "snap," often triggered by excessive pressure on a person's mental health, leads to a breakdown and eventual collapse—so I have been told. The final outcome is often imprisonment.

Then there are the system-manufactured "crimes," such as failing a drug test, missing a curfew, traveling without consent, associating with others on parole when you're on parole (state-sanctioned slaves are not allowed to congregate outside prison), missing an appointment with a freedom supervisor, failing to pay a parking ticket, and countless other misdemeanors that label a person as a criminal.

This book has transformed my understanding of the history of mass incarceration and its impact on Black women. It has also changed my perspective on crime. I now view those labeled as "criminals" as victims of a society that projects its failures onto them and conceals its own harm. This harm, manifested in the suffering of individuals, remains trapped behind tall brick walls, gun towers, barbed wire, heavy steel doors, iron bars, and ill-fitted uniforms marking their status as property. But beneath the denim blues, orange jumpsuits, and stripes are individuals, each with unique purpose. I do not believe anyone should be judged by the worst thing they've ever done, and I often wonder what might occur if society recognized people's humanity beyond their conviction. What if we chose love over punishment? What if we made love the path to freedom?

Making love the solution to freedom means creating safe spaces for women to heal after their incarceration. It means ensuring their new home is not an extension of prison through the state-issued rules that, if broken, could result in being reported and sent back to jail or prison. It means feeling safe, building community, discovering one's purpose, and contributing significantly to society. It means empowering women by training them to be leaders and to use their stories to drive change.

A New Way of Life Reentry Project is leading the freedom movement by creating opportunities for formerly incarcerated women to help change the world. The organization's SAFE Housing Network is a primary example of how Black women are leading the fight to liberate women from state sanctioned slavery and bring them into safe houses they can call home. This national collective of formerly incarcerated women is decarcerating America one home at a time. Since its founding in 2018, fifty members across the United States have established thirty-seven homes.

A New Way of Life is also investing in formerly incarcerated women through its national leadership training program, Women Organizing for Justice and Opportunity. This six-month program helps formerly incarcerated women hone their social justice leadership skills. It is training generations of formerly incarcerated leaders.

The National Council for Incarcerated and Formerly Incarcerated Women and Girls is another national organization leading the movement for justice. The council is committed to abolishing incarceration for women and girls. Through annual conferences, research, and courageous advocacy, this organization is advancing the freedom fight and inspiring women across America to get involved.

One of the joys of writing this book has been meeting—and joining the work of—members of these organizations, as well as other national and local groups. They include the National Black Women's Justice Institute; the Formerly Incarcerated, Convicted People & Families Movement; the Southern Center for Human Rights; the Kemba Smith Foundation; and local organizations such as Lending Hands (Virginia), the RECH Foundation (Mississippi), True Beginnings (Nevada), Women on the Rise GA (Georgia), Life After Release (Maryland), and Win Recovery (Illinois).

It is inspiring to join hands with formerly incarcerated people who are participating in their own liberation. History has shown that the systems that created slavery's mass incarceration are incapable of repairing it. Thus, it is our collective responsibility to ensure a free world for those currently in chains and to prevent future generations from experiencing enslavement.

In addition to the brave efforts of formerly incarcerated individuals to promote freedom and justice, here are my proposals for achieving true freedom. Breaking the barriers to freedom, to me, means abolishing state-sanctioned slavery and removing the Thirteenth Amendment's exception clause from the US Constitution; decriminalizing trauma, addiction, poverty, mental unwellness, and Black skin; banning the Black box and the discrimination that follows in the form of voting disenfranchisement, housing bias, educational barriers, and job discrimination; dismantling social stigmas that limit formerly incarcerated people; ensuring equal access to freedom and first-class citizenship for descendants of the enslaved; providing federally funded reentry support controlled by the people; abolishing supervised freedom; and providing poor families with the financial resources necessary to stay together rather than investing in a system that tears them apart.

For me, the solution for freedom is love and righteous action.

ACKNOWLEDGMENTS

My faith in God made this book possible, along with the people I believe He has placed in my life to assist me in this process. I have received tremendous support throughout my seven-year journey of writing *Searching for Jane Crow*, and I am grateful for the chance to publicly acknowledge each of you.

Gayatri Patnaik, words cannot express how thankful I am to have had the opportunity to develop this book with you. Thank you for showing me grace when I needed it, and for gently encouraging me along the way. Your visionary leadership, kindness, and patience are appreciated more than you realize.

Daina Ramey Berry, thank you for encouraging me to pursue this project from the beginning. I am grateful for your time, resources, and wisdom shared with me over the years—and so much more. Your friendship is a gift and a blessing.

Jana Sanchez, I greatly appreciate your invaluable assistance in helping me translate and communicate my ideas more effectively throughout the writing process of this book. Cecelia Cancellaro, I also thank you for reading early drafts of *Jane Crow*, and for lending your editorial expertise to this work.

If it takes a village to raise a child, then I believe the same applies to a book. Thank you to my wonderful colleagues who have helped nurture this book by providing advice in the research and writing process, sharing sources, offering a sounding board for ideas, and for always being so kind and generous overall. These individuals include Derrick E. White, Jelani Favors, Mary Ellen Curtin, Robert Chase, Dennis Childs, Robert Vinson, Sheila Curran Bernard, Sharon Harley, Ashley D. Farmer, Marlene Daut, Adam Clulow, Nathalie Rech, Telisha Dionne Bailey, Tara Dudley, Vanessa Holden, Jennifer Guglielmo, Camille Westmont, Chassidy Olainu-Alade, Sam Collins III, Annette Rodriguez, Alan Tully, Amanda White Gibson, Shay Price, Charlene Fletcher, and Nicole D. Porter.

Kali Nicole Gross and Cheryl D. Hicks, I remain forever grateful for the foundation you have laid in studying the history of incarcerated Black women, and for daring to explore the experiences of those who have been forgotten or deemed unworthy of being remembered.

Signe Forumy, my *Jane Crow* writing experience would not have been the same without you. Thank you for being a devoted friend, thought partner, and for adding so much joy and levity to my life in Austin, Texas.

To my sisters in faith who have prayed me out of some valleys, helped me create structures to facilitate my work (and rest), made me laugh *hard*, showered me with kindness, and just let me be me: Tara McDuffey, Alicia Shivers, Regis Fox, Amy Tillerson-Brown, Anika Clark, Nicole Spivey, Breanna Gray, Ava Purkiss, Tamitha Middleton, thank you!

To my research assistants, Joshua Crutchfield, Jaden Janak, Alyssa Peterson, Diana Heredia, Keiara Price, Safa Michigan, Claire Corkish, Madeleine Gravely, and Zari Taylor, I am thankful for the incredible work you did to help uncover many of the stories featured in *Jane Crow*. Safa, I especially appreciate your efforts in helping me get over the hump.

Courtney Meador, thank you for your last-minute technical assistance when I needed it and for your overall generosity. I appreciate you.

One of the most cherished experiences I have had in writing this book has involved building community with some of the world's brightest leaders and justice seekers. Susan Burton, meeting you has been one of the greatest gifts I have ever received. I have learned so much from you over the years and appreciate our friendship more each day. Kemba Smith-Pradia, doing life and justice work with you has been one of the highlights of my *Jane Crow* journey. I am grateful for the bond we share.

I would like to further express my gratitude to the formerly incarcerated Black women leaders, as well as the justice seekers without lived experience, whom I have had the privilege to collaborate with through my Black Women and Mass Incarceration Internship Project at The University of Texas at Austin and the University of Virginia. Thank you for teaching my students the importance of supporting justice-involved individuals and inspiring them to make a meaningful difference in the world. These changemakers include Andrea James, Sydney McKinney, Pauline Rogers, Marilynn Winn, Robyn Hasan, Qiana Johnson, Vera Moore, Cherry Henley, Bethany Little, Carmen Johnson, Cynthia Simons, and Cheryl Ward.

Writing *Jane Crow* has shown me how crucial the insights of formerly incarcerated and system-impacted experts are to understanding this history. I want to thank the experts who generously shared their stories with me, enlightening my perspective on an epidemic that I partially understood. These individuals include Denise Coleman, Andrea Carter, Veronica Hester, Erica Thomas, Summer Pichon, Kyndia Riley, Myesha Johnson, Georgia Horton, Geneva Cooley, Patricia Washington, Karen Hernandez, Annette Strain, Stephanie J., Selena Lopez, Diane Figueroa, Kimberly Dunne, Asia Johnson, Gizell Hayes, Jean Boone, Latrice Kemp-Jones, Shamica Neal, Shuntay Weston, Stephanie Lilly, and Xavier Jones.

This book would not have been possible without the generous financial support of the Andrew Carnegie Foundation, the Institute for Historical Studies at The University of Texas at Austin, and the College of Arts and Sciences and the Office of the Executive Vice President and Provost at the University of Virginia. Thank you for investing in this work and in the lives of those it will impact.

I would like to extend my heartfelt gratitude to the archivists and staff at the following institutions: the Library of Virginia, Virginia Museum of History & Culture, Valentine Museum, Texas State Library and Archives Commission, Harry Ransom Center, Dolph Briscoe Center for American History, Kentucky Department for Library and Archives, Georgia Archives, City of Savannah Municipal Archives, Library of Congress,

Tennessee State Library and Archives, Mississippi Department of Archives and History, Washington, DC Office of Public Records, Maryland State Archives, Texas Prison Museum, and the Jimmy Carter Presidential Library and Museum. Your invaluable assistance is greatly appreciated.

To my mother, Evonne LeFlouria, I love you and thank God for you. Thank you for setting an early example of selfless service and sacrificial generosity. Everything I know about helping others I first learned from you.

To my brothers, Andre and Melvin LeFlouria, with every passing day I love you more . . .

And to the One who covers my life, carries me through every challenging season and trial, and provides the foundation upon which I stand, I forever give you praise.

IMAGE CREDITS

(Delia Garlic): Library of Congress, Manuscript Division, Washington, DC.

(Enslaved woman in a slave jail): Civil War photographs, 1861–1865, Library of Congress, Prints and Photographs Division, Washington, DC.

(Fanny Jackson and children): *Slave Market of America* (1836), Library of Congress, Rare Book and Special Collections Division, Washington, DC.

(Jail commitment notification for capture of Thursday): *Wilmington Journal*, December 31, 1850.

(Advertisement for sale of Harriet Purdy): *Annapolis Gazette*, December 20, 1866.

(Mary Morst): Library of Virginia, Richmond, VA.

(Women prisoners at Goree): Courtesy of the Texas Prison Museum, Huntsville, TX.

(Mary Prince and Amy Carter): National Archives and Records Administration, Jimmy Carter Library and Museum, Atlanta, GA.

NOTES

INTRODUCTION: BLACK WOMEN, MASS INCARCERATION, AND THE LEGACIES OF SLAVERY

1. Michelle Alexander, *The New Jim Crow: Mass Incarceration in the Age of Colorblindness* (New York: The New Press, 2010), 2.
2. The term "Jane Crow" was first introduced in 1947 by American activist and lawyer Pauli Murray to describe the unique and intersecting forms of discrimination faced by Black women, resulting from both racism and sexism. My use of the term, however, differs significantly from Murray's in that it emphasizes race rather than sexism as the central aspect of Black women's oppression.
3. Daina Ramey Berry and Kali Nicole Gross, *A Black Women's History of the United States* (Boston: Beacon Press, 2020), 4.
4. It is important to note that some enslaved women were committed to jail by their enslavers for "safekeeping" when they traveled. Voluntary confinement also occurred when enslavers took their enslaved laborers to jail to be whipped.
5. Berry and Gross, *A Black Women's History of the United States*, 52.
6. I primarily use "chattel history" to apply to free Black women who were born enslaved. However, it also applies to free Black women who never experienced enslavement but suffered its effects.
7. Black women became free in other ways, including being purchased by family members, friends, antislavery activists, or abolitionists. Others became free when their enslavers died or when they were legally manumitted.
8. Martha S. Jones, "Why Republicans Keep Calling for the End of Birthright Citizenship: It's About More Than Immigration," *The Atlantic*, July 2, 2023. https://www.theatlantic.com/ideas/archive/2023/07/birthright-citizenship-trump-desantis-2024/674583/. See also Martha S. Jones, *Birthright Citizens: A History of Race and Rights in Antebellum America* (Cambridge: Cambridge University Press, 2018).

CHAPTER 1: FINDING JANE CROW

1. "Testimony of Delia Garlic," *Federal Writers' Project: Slave Narrative Project*, vol. 1, Alabama, 1936–1938, Library of Congress, Washington, DC.

2. "Testimony of Delia Garlic."
3. "Testimony of Delia Garlic."
4. Examples of scholarship examining the history of Black incarceration during the antebellum period includes Glenn McNair, *Criminal Injustice: Slaves and Free Blacks in Georgia's Criminal Justice System* (Charlottesville: University of Virginia Press, 2009); Michele Lise Tarter and Richard Bell, eds., *Buried Lives: Incarcerated in Early America* (Athens: University of Georgia Press, 2012); Rashauna Johnson, *Slavery's Metropolis: Unfree Labor in New Orleans During the Age of Revolutions* (Cambridge: Cambridge University Press, 2018); Jeff Forrett, *Williams' Gang: A Notorious Slave Trader and His Cargo of Black Convicts* (Cambridge: Cambridge University Press, 2020); John K. Bardes, *The Carceral City: Slavery and the Making of Mass Incarceration in New Orleans, 1803–1930* (Chapel Hill: University of North Carolina Press, 2024); and Kelly Birch and Thomas C. Buchanan, "The Penalty of a Tyrant's Law: Landscapes of Incarceration During the Second Slavery," *Slavery & Abolition* 34, no. 1 (2013): 22–38.
5. VA City Sergeant Register, March 13, 1841–May 8, 1846, Virginia Museum of History & Culture, Richmond, VA; Nancy Frantel, *Richmond, Virginia Uncovered: The Records of Slaves and Free Blacks Listed in the City Sergeant Jail Register, 1841–1846* (Westminster, MD: Heritage Books, 2019), 104.
6. This calculation is based on information from Measuring Worth, www.measuringworth.com, which provides historical data on economic aggregates.
7. Frantel, *Richmond, Virginia Uncovered*, 104.
8. Henry Bibb, *Narrative of the Life and Adventures of Henry Bibb, an American Slave, Written by Himself* (1849), 40–41, Documenting the American South, University of North Carolina at Chapel Hill, https://docsouth.unc.edu/neh/bibb/bibb.html.
9. Bibb, *Narrative of the Life and Adventures of Henry Bibb*, 37–38.
10. Bibb, *Narrative of the Life and Adventures of Henry Bibb*, 42–43.
11. Bibb, *Narrative of the Life and Adventures of Henry Bibb*, 91.
12. Bibb, *Narrative of the Life and Adventures of Henry Bibb*, 92.
13. Bibb, *Narrative of the Life and Adventures of Henry Bibb*, 93.
14. For further reading on the history of the domestic slave trade, see Steven Deyle, *Carry Me Back: The Domestic Slave Trade in American Life* (Oxford: Oxford University Press, 2006); Forrett, *Williams' Gang*; Walter Johnson, *Soul by Soul: Inside the Antebellum Slave Market* (Cambridge, MA: Harvard University Press, 1999); Calvin Schermerhorn, *The Business of Slavery and the Rise of American Capitalism* (New Haven, CT: Yale University Press, 2015); and Edward E. Baptist, *The Half Has Never Been Told: Slavery and the Making of American Capitalism* (New York: Basic Books, 2016).
15. Maurie D. McInnis, "Slave Pens, Slave Jails, and Slave Markets," in *World of a Slave: Encyclopedia of the Material Life of Slaves in the United States*, ed. Martha B. Katz-Hyman and Kym S. Rice (Santa Barbara: Greenwood Press, 2010), 464.
16. The 1830 US Federal Census shows 145 enslaved people at the Franklin and Armfield jail in Alexandria. The breakdown is as follows: 71 men and boys (one

under ten years old, 50 between ten and twenty-four years old, and 20 between twenty-four and thirty-six years old) and 74 women and girls (four under ten years old, 50 between ten and twenty-four years old, and 20 between twenty-four and thirty-six years old), from 1830 US Federal Census, Ancestry.com, Lehi, UT: Ancestry.com Operations Inc., 2010, https://www.ancestry.com.

17. Ethan Allen Andrews, *Slavery and the Domestic Slave-Trade in the United States* (Boston: Light & Stearns, 1836), 141.
18. Edward Baptist, "'Cuffy,' 'Fancy Maids,' and 'One-Eyed Men': Rape, Commodification, and the Domestic Slave Trade in the United States," *American Historical Review* 106, no. 5 (December 2001): 1620. For further reading, see Brenda E. Stevenson, "What's Love Got to Do with It? Concubinage and Enslaved Women and Girls in the Antebellum South," *Journal of African American History* 98, no. 1 (Winter 2013): 99–125.
19. Sarah H. Bradford, *Scenes in the Life of Harriet Tubman* (Auburn, NY: W. J. Moses, Printer, 1869), 14, 16, 58, Documenting the American South, https://docsouth.unc.edu/neh/bradford/bradford.html.
20. Isabel Howell, "John Armfield, Slave-Trader," *Tennessee Historical Quarterly* 2, no. 1 (March 1943): 20.
21. McInnis, "Slave Pens, Slave Jails, and Slave Markets," 468.
22. Bibb, *Narrative of the Life and Adventures of Henry Bibb*, 103.
23. George P. Rawick, ed., *The American Slave: Texas Narratives*, vol. 5, parts 3 and 4 (Westport, CT: Greenwood Press, 1972).
24. Daina Ramey Berry, *The Price for Their Pound of Flesh: The Value of the Enslaved, from Womb to Grave, in the Building of a Nation* (Boston: Beacon Press, 2017), 33, 51, 58.
25. Josiah Henson, *Truth Stranger Than Fiction: Father Henson's Story of His Own Life* (1858; repr., Chapel Hill: University Library, University of North Carolina at Chapel Hill, 2000), 13, Documenting the American South, https://docsouth.unc.edu/neh/henson58/henson58.html.
26. Register of Slave Commitments to the DC Jail, 1848–1862, accession no. D.C.A. 97–01, Washington, DC, Office of Public Records, District of Columbia, hereafter cited as DCPR. Eliza's delivery was assisted by "Dr. Mather," the jail's physician. In August 1849, one month after she escaped, her enslaver located her at the jail and paid $11.20 to cover the cost of her confinement.
27. *Slave Market of America*, New York, American Anti-Slavery Society, 1836, Library of Congress, http://hdl.loc.gov/loc.pnp/ppmsca.19705; Register of Commitments to the DC Jail for Criminal Offences ["Criminal Docket"], vol. 1, Aug. 1850–July 1855, DCPR.
28. *Proceedings and Acts of the Maryland General Assembly*, 1796.
29. Fanny Jackson, Louisa Jackson, Robert Jackson, and Maria Jackson v. Ariss Buckner and Bernard H. Buckner, in *O Say Can You See: Early Washington, D.C., Law & Family*, ed. William G. Thomas III et al. (University of Nebraska–Lincoln), http://earlywashingtondc.org/cases/oscys.caseid.0461.
30. *Slave Market of America*, 1836.

31. This information is derived from the Register of Slave Commitments to the DC Jail, 1848–1862, DCPR.
32. Wilma King, *The Essence of Liberty: Free Black Women During the Slave Era* (Columbia: University of Missouri Press, 2006), 64. It is important to note that during this period, 1,299 enslaved women and 947 enslaved men also resided in Baltimore, according to statistics provided in King's work. For a comprehensive reading on free Black women's lives in Maryland, see Jessica Millward, *Finding Charity's Folk: Enslaved and Free Black Women in Maryland* (Athens: University of Georgia Press, 2015). Another relevant reading on free Black women's lives and labors in antebellum America is Erica Armstrong Dunbar, *A Fragile Freedom: African American Women and Emancipation in the Antebellum City* (New Haven, CT: Yale University Press, 2011).
33. Baltimore City Jail Runaway Docket, 1836–1850, Reel 79170, CM1352–2; 1850–1864, Reel 79171–1, CM1352–3, Maryland State Archives, Annapolis, Maryland, hereafter cited as MSA.
34. New Orleans Register of Chained Slaves Employed in Public Works, vol. 3 (1827–1835), New Orleans, Louisiana, US, Early Police Records, 1805–1865, Lehi, UT: Ancestry.com Operations Inc., 2023, https://www.ancestry.com.
35. New Orleans Police Jail—Registers of Chained Slaves Employed in the Public Works, 1820–1851, Microfilm TX430, vol. 2, New Orleans Public Library, City Archives & Special Collections, New Orleans, LA; Louis Philippe de Roffignac, "Voucher in French for Work Done by Negro Slave in the Chain Gang" (Voucher, New Orleans, November 12, 1822), https://jstor.org/stable/community.31030970; Denis Prieur, "Voucher in French for Work Done by Negro Slave in the Chain Gang" (Voucher, New Orleans, December 10, 1829), https://jstor.org/stable/community.31030694.
36. *Wilmington Journal*, Wilmington, NC, October 24, 1851; *Charleston Courier*, Charleston, SC, February 12, 1825; *Milledgeville Federal Union*, Milledgeville, GA, April 20, 1858. Runaway ads often included the names and descriptions of escaped slaves, including physical features, literacy level, specialized skills, and location where an enslaved person might be headed. These ads represent an early form of racial profiling.
37. *Mobile Register*, Mobile, AL, November 15, 1832.
38. Charles Emery Stevens, *Anthony Burns: A History* (Boston: J. P. Jewett Co., 1856), 191. In 1854, Anthony Burns escaped from a Virginia plantation to Boston. He was captured under the Fugitive Slave Act of 1850 and tried in court. His case drew national publicity and sparked protests. But Burns was returned to slavery.
39. Stevens, *Anthony Burns*, 188.
40. Stevens, *Anthony Burns*; Charles H. Corey, *A History of the Richmond Theological Seminary with Reminiscences of Thirty Years' Work Among the Colored People of the South* (Richmond, VA: J. W. Randolph, Co., 1895), 75–76. The jail compound owned by Robert Lumpkin originally belonged to Bacon Tait, a slave dealer. In

1833, Tait deeded the property to Lewis A. Collier, a fellow Richmond trader. After the Bank of Virginia seized the land from Collier, Lumpkin took possession of it. For further reading, see Matthew R. Laird, *Archaeological Data Recovery Investigation of the Lumpkin's Slave Jail Site (44HE1053)*, vol. 1, Research Report, Williamsburg, VA, James River Institute for Archaeology, Inc., August 2010.

41. Stevens, *Anthony Burns*, 50.
42. 1840 US Federal Census, free schedule, Richmond Ward 1, Henrico County, Virginia, 561, National Archives Microfilm T623, roll 149, Ancestry.com, Lehi, UT: Ancestry.com Operations Inc., 2010, https://www.ancestry.com.
43. Corey, *A History of the Richmond Theological Seminary*, 48; Sydney Trent, "She Was Raped by the Owner of a Notorious Slave Jail. Later, She Inherited It," *Washington Post*, February 1, 2020, https://www.washingtonpost.com/history/2020/02/02/lumpkin-slave-rape-richmond-jail/; Hannah Catherine Craddock, "Black Female Landowners in Richmond, Virginia, 1850–1877" (master's thesis, William & Mary, 2012).
44. Lumpkin Jail Ledger (1849–1850), Valentine Museum, Richmond, VA.
45. Lumpkin Jail Ledger.
46. "Testimony of Virginia Hayes Shepherd," in Charles L. Perdue Jr., Thomas E. Barden, and Robert K. Phillips, eds., *Weevils in the Wheat: Interviews with Virginia Ex-Slaves* (Charlottesville: University Press of Virginia, 1991), 257.
47. Darlene Clark Hine and Kathleen Thompson, *A Shining Thread of Hope: The History of Black Women in America* (New York: Broadway Books, 1998), 171.
48. In 1662, the Virginia General Assembly passed an act that determined that all children born in the colony—including those born from interracial sex—would "be held bond or free according to the condition of the mother." Heredity as a basis for enslavement was adopted in every slaveholding territory.
49. Corey, *A History of the Richmond Theological Seminary*, 48.
50. Corey, *A History of the Richmond Theological Seminary*, 77.
51. John J. Zaborney, *Slaves for Hire: Renting Enslaved Laborers in Antebellum Virginia* (Baton Rouge: Louisiana State University Press, 2012), 141. See also Jonathan D. Martin, *Divided Mastery: Slave Hiring in the American South* (Cambridge, MA: Harvard University Press, 2004).
52. "Adjudged a Slave," *Richmond Enquirer*, November 25, 1853.
53. Sally E. Hadden, *Slave Patrols: Law and Violence in Virginia and the Carolinas* (Cambridge, MA: Harvard University Press, 2001), 4.
54. As quoted in Hadden, *Slave Patrols*, 63.
55. An Act to Amend the Several Laws Concerning Slaves, 1806, Virginia General Assembly, https://www.encyclopediavirginia.org/_An_ACT_to_amend_the_several_laws_concerning_slaves_1806.
56. In 1826, the sheriff replaced the overseer of the poor as the selling agent for free Black individuals who remained in Virginia, contrary to the 1806 law. Proceeds from the sale of formerly enslaved people were distributed by the county to offer aid to people who were impoverished, elderly, disabled, widowed,

orphaned, or otherwise in need. An individual had to be considered "deserving" of assistance. Free Blacks were rarely deemed worthy of relief.

57. "Adjudged a Slave," *Richmond Enquirer*, 1853.
58. Frantel, *Richmond, Virginia Uncovered*, 17. Four enslaved laborers and ten "free colored persons" experienced confinement at Spraggins's property according to the 1840 US Federal Census, Ancestry.com, Lehi, UT: Ancestry.com Operations Inc., 2010. For further reading on the practice of selling Black women for unpaid jail fees, see Amanda White Gibson, "Neither Slave nor Free: Black Jail Debt Peonage in Antebellum Virginia, 1841–1846," *Journal of Southern History* 89, no. 4 (November 2023): 629–58.
59. *Proceedings and Acts of the Maryland General Assembly*, 1796.
60. "Slave-Catching in Washington," *Evening Post*, March 4, 1862.
61. "Slave-Catching in Washington."
62. Frantel, *Richmond, Virginia Uncovered*, 16.
63. *Report of the Board of Directors of the Penitentiary of the State of Louisiana* (New Orleans: Emile La Sere, State Printer, 1853), 4, 7, 16, 17.
64. Kerry Myers, "Bad Girls, Convict Women: A Historical Look at Women in the Louisiana Penal System," *The Angolite* 36, no. 6 (November/December 2011): 47. See also Jeff Forrett, "Before Angola: Enslaved Prisoners in the Louisiana State Penitentiary," *Louisiana History: The Journal of the Louisiana Historical Association* 54, no. 2 (Spring 2013): 133–71.
65. The 1823 Code Noir (slave code) of Louisiana allowed the substitution of life imprisonment at hard labor for the death penalty. This may explain why fewer women were executed than one might expect based on regional trends.
66. Ten enslaved women gave birth in the prison. Some, if not all, of them experienced rape. These assaults produced eleven children, all of whom were taken from their mother and auctioned on the courthouse steps for a total of $7,591. The proceeds from these sales went into the "free school fund," which paid to educate white children at no cost. All information regarding the incarceration of enslaved women at the Louisiana State Penitentiary, as well as the sale of their children, is drawn from Brett Derbes, "'Secret Horrors': Enslaved Women and Children in the Louisiana State Penitentiary, 1833–1862," *Journal of African American History* 98, no. 2 (Spring 2013): 277–90.

CHAPTER 2: FREEDOM'S AFTERMATH

1. The testimony of Bongy Jackson as quoted in Lyle Saxon, Edward Dreyer, and Robert Tallant, eds., *Gumbo Ya-Ya: A Collection of Louisiana Folk Tales* (Boston: Houghton Mifflin Company, 1945), 239. See also Tyler D. Parry, "The Holy Land of Matrimony: The Complex Legacy of the Broomstick Wedding in American History," *American Studies* 55, no. 1 (2016): 81–106.
2. For further reading on the Freedmen's Bureau, see Mary Farmer-Kaiser, *Freedwomen and the Freedmen's Bureau: Race, Gender, & Public Policy in the Age of Emancipation* (New York: Fordham University Press, 2010); Paul A. Cimbala,

Under the Guardianship of the Nation: The Freedmen's Bureau and the Reconstruction of Georgia, 1865–1870 (Athens: University of Georgia Press, 2003); and Claude F. Oubre, *Forty Acres and a Mule: The Freedmen's Bureau and Black Landownership* (Baton Rouge: Louisiana State University Press, 1978).

3. According to South Carolina law, no "person of color" could "pursue or practice the art, trade or business of an artisan, mechanic or shopkeeper, or any other trade, employment or business besides that of husbandry, or that of a servant under a contract for service or labor on his own account and for his own benefit . . . until he shall have a license therefore from the judge of the District Court; which license shall be good for one year only." From "An Act to Establish and Regulate the Domestic Relations of Persons of Color and to Amend the Law in Relation to Paupers and Vagrancy," Act No. 4733, South Carolina General Assembly, December 19, 1865. In *The Statutes at Large of South Carolina*, vol. 12: *Acts from December 1861 to December 1866* (Columbia: Republican Printing Corp., 1875), 279.
4. In 1870, the Fifteenth Amendment was ratified. It provided that "the right of citizens of the United States to vote shall not be denied or abridged by the United States or by any State on account of race, color, or previous condition of servitude."
5. Before the ratification of the Fourteenth Amendment, states had laws preventing people with felony convictions from voting. However, following the ratification of the Fifteenth Amendment, many Southern states increased their use of felony disenfranchisement laws to prevent Black men from voting.
6. "Memphis Riot and Massacres," in *Black Women in White America: A Documentary History*, ed. Gerda Lerner (New York: Vintage Books, 1992), 174–75. Originally published as US House of Representatives, *Report of the Committee on the Memphis Riots*, 39th Cong., 1st sess., House Report 101 (1866).
7. Anonymous, *The Independent* 54, no. 2807 (September 18, 1902): 2221–24. For further reading, see Crystal Lynn Webster, *Raising Racists: The Socialization of White Children in the Jim Crow South* (Lexington: University Press of Kentucky, 2011).
8. "Appearance Docket," May 12, 1911, Internet Archive, https://web.archive.org/web/20190708143928/http://lauranelsonlynching.weebly.com/uploads/6/4/5/5/6455077/austin_nelson_jail_charges_2.jpg.
9. "Negro Female Prisoner Gets Unruly," *Okemah Ledger*, May 18, 1911.
10. "Lynchers Avenge the Murder of Geo. Loney," *Oklahoma Ledger*, May 25, 1911. Photographs of Laura and Lawrence Nelson's bodies hanging from a bridge, with dozens of spectators appearing in the background, were circulated as souvenir postcards. These photographs are accessible through Without Sanctuary: Lynching Photography in America, https://withoutsanctuary.org/.
11. Between 1865 and 1950, over six thousand Black women, men, and children were lynched. These casualties include formerly enslaved people, their children, and their grandchildren. See *Reconstruction in America: Racial Violence After*

the Civil War, 1865–1876, Equal Justice Initiative, 2020, https://eji.org/report/reconstruction-in-america/. This report documents nearly two thousand lynchings of Black people by white mobs during the Reconstruction era (1865–1877) and raises the total number of reported lynchings to roughly 6,500 from the end of the Civil War to 1950. But multiple generations of American descendants of slavery have since died on the battleground of racial terror: Sandra Bland, Breonna Taylor, Trayvon Martin, Michael Brown, Ahmaud Arbery, and George Floyd, to name a few.

12. A Negro Nurse, "More Slavery at the South," *The Independent* 72, no. 3295 (January 25, 1912): 196–200.
13. A Negro Nurse, "More Slavery at the South."
14. For a comprehensive study of Black washerwomen in the urban South, see Tera Hunter, *To 'Joy My Freedom: Southern Black Women's Lives and Labors After the Civil War* (Cambridge, MA: Harvard University Press, 1997).
15. The first scholarly discussion of Harriet Purdy's story appears in Dennis Childs, *Slaves of the State: Black Incarceration from the Chain Gang to the Penitentiary* (Minneapolis: University of Minnesota Press, 2015), 58–59. It also appears in primary sources such as *Fraser's Magazine for Town and Country* 75 (London: Longmans, Green, and Co., 1867), 259.
16. "Public Sale," *Annapolis Gazette*, December 20, 1866.
17. Owen M. Taylor, *The History of Annapolis, the Capital of Maryland: The State House, Its Various Public Buildings . . . Together with a Full History and Description of the United States Naval Academy from Its Origin to the Present Time* (Baltimore: Turnbull Brothers, 1872).
18. Rick Rojas, "Leaving Prison at 72," *New York Times*, October 28, 2019, https://www.nytimes.com/2019/10/28/us/geneva-cooley-alabama-prison.html; Matt Taibbi, "Cruel and Unusual Punishment: The Shame of Three Strikes Laws," *Rolling Stone*, March 27, 2013.
19. Helen Nguyen, "Law & Disorder: Our Right to a Speedy Trial Stands, Even During a Pandemic," *Daily Trojan*, October 4, 2021. See also US Constitution, Amendment VI: "In all criminal prosecutions, the accused shall enjoy the right to a speedy and public trial . . . [and] to have the Assistance of Counsel for his defense."
20. Elijah L. Rockhold is listed as a farmer in the 1870 US Federal Census, population schedule, Lehi, UT: Ancestry.com Operations Inc., 2009, https://www.ancestry.com. In 1860, he owned seventeen enslaved people: two women, two girls, six men, and seven boys, the youngest only a year old, according to the 1860 US Federal Census, slave schedules, Ancestry.com, Lehi, UT: Ancestry.com Operations Inc., 2010, https://www.ancestry.com.
21. Harriet Purdy appears in the 1880 US Federal Census, population schedule, as "head of household" and mother of three children: Maggie (nine), George (six), and Hattie (two). No occupation is listed for her. See 1880 US Federal Census, population schedule, Ancestry.com, Lehi, UT: Ancestry.com Operations Inc., 2010, https://www.ancestry.com.

CHAPTER 3: DEBT SLAVERY

1. "Vagrant Negroes Sold at Auction," *Tucson Citizen*, December 3, 1902; "Negroes Sold on Block as Kentucky Vagrants," *Salt Lake Telegram*, December 3, 1902.
2. "Off Their Muscles," *New York Herald*, March 20, 1887; "Selling White Men," *Savannah Morning News*, March 27, 1887.
3. *Savannah Morning News*, March 27, 1887.
4. *Tucson Citizen* and *Salt Lake Telegram*, December 3, 1902.
5. *The General Statutes of Kentucky: As Compiled by Edward I. Bullock, James M. Nesbitt, and George W. Craddock; and Adopted by the General Assembly by an Act Approved April 22, 1873* (Frankfort: Kentucky Yeoman Office, Major, Johnston & Barrett, 1881).
6. For an example, see "A Negro Advertised for Sale in Maryland," *Providence Evening Press*, December 10, 1866.
7. "Rear Guards of Slavery," *New York Tribune*, December 28, 1866.
8. "Public Sale," *Annapolis Gazette*, December 20, 1866; "The Civil Rights Bill in Maryland—Selling Negroes for Crime," *Daily National Intelligencer*, December 25, 1866.
9. "Untitled," *Duluth News-Tribune*, May 8, 1885.
10. "The Vagrant Law," *Daily Inter Ocean*, April 27, 1892; "Sale of Negro Labor: Colored Men and Women Put on the Auction Block," *Topeka Call*, June 5, 1892; "Negroes Sold at Auction," *Fort Morgan Times*, May 6, 1892.
11. In her freedom suit, Winny argued that her enslaver, Phebe Whitesides, took her from Kentucky to Indiana Territory, where slavery was prohibited. Twenty years later, Phebe continued to enslave Winny, even though she had been legally freed by living on free soil.
12. This estimate is based on calculations provided in Douglas A. Blackmon, *Slavery by Another Name: The Re-Enslavement of Black Americans from the Civil War to World War II* (New York: Anchor, 2009). While it is impossible to determine the exact number of individuals enslaved from the post–Civil War period to World War II, Blackmon estimates that the figure could be in the millions.
13. "Negroes at Auction," *Jackson Citizen*, December 21, 1880; "Sold into Slavery," *Chicago Daily Tribune*, December 19, 1880.
14. For a detailed explanation of how enslaved people were valued and rated according to their physical strength and skill, see Daina Ramey Berry, "'We'm Fus' Rate Bargain': Value, Labor, and Price in a Georgia Slave Community," in *The Chattel Principle: Internal Slave Trades in the Americas*, ed. Walter Johnson (New Haven, CT: Yale University Press, 2008), 55–71.
15. *Jackson Citizen*, December 21, 1880; *Chicago Daily Tribune*, December 19, 1880.
16. For a comprehensive history of debt peonage, see Pete Daniel, *The Shadow of Slavery: Peonage in the South, 1901–1969* (Urbana: University of Illinois Press, 1972).
17. "Sold Negroes to the Highest Bidder," *Mexico Missouri Message*, July 16, 1903.
18. "Slavery in the South," *Leader-Post*, August 27, 1903.

19. "Slavery in the South."
20. "Slavery in the South."
21. "Slavery in the South."
22. "Slavery in the South."
23. Blackmon, *Slavery by Another Name*, 146–47.
24. Blackmon, *Slavery by Another Name*, 146.
25. Blackmon, *Slavery by Another Name*.
26. James Monroe Smith's peonage practices are well-documented in E. Merton Coulter's *James Monroe Smith: Georgia Planter, Before Death and After* (Athens: University of Georgia Press, 2002).
27. "The New Slavery in the South—An Autobiography: A Georgia Negro Peon," *The Independent* 56, no. 2807 (February 25, 1904): 409–14.
28. *The Peonage Files of the U.S. Department of Justice, 1901–1945, Black Studies Research Series*, microfilm collection (Frederick, MD: University Publications of America, 1989), reel 1, frame 0643, as cited in La Toya Tanisha Francis and Patrick Rael, "Mentha Morrison: A Story of Debt Peonage in Jim Crow Georgia," *Black Perspectives*, October 4, 2018, https://www.aaihs.org/mentha-morrison-a-story-of-debt-peonage-in-jim-crow-georgia/.
29. Mentha Morrison to Theodore Roosevelt, *The Peonage Files of the U.S. Department of Justice, 1901–1945* (microfilm), ed. Pete Daniel, DOJ Case No. 3098–1902, quoted in Dennis Childs, *Slaves of the State: Black Incarceration from the Chain Gang to the Penitentiary* (Minneapolis: University of Minnesota Press, 2015), 184.
30. "Two Pardons Granted," *Montgomery Advertiser*, November 6, 1901; "Sheriff May Is Accused," *Montgomery Advertiser*, June 11, 1904.
31. *Montgomery Advertiser*, June 11, 1904; *Montgomery Advertiser*, November 6, 1901.
32. "Modern Day Plantations with Antoinette Harrell," *Research at the National Archives and Beyond* (podcast), July 2, 2015.
33. "Usual Calm Before Storm with Police," *Macon Telegraph*, May 9, 1915.
34. "Raid Negro Women, Solve Cook Problem," *Macon Telegraph*, December 2, 1912.
35. Hunter, *To 'Joy My Freedom*, 88–89.
36. "The Corner Talk," *Macon Telegraph*, March 20, 1891; Talitha L. LeFlouria, *Chained in Silence: Black Women and Convict Labor in the New South* (Chapel Hill: University of North Carolina Press, 2015), 177.
37. Atlanta Police Department, Court Docket, vol. 1, 1886–87, MSS 787, Kenan Research Center at the Atlanta History Center, Atlanta, GA; Police Department, Criminal Registers, 1873–74, 1877, City of Savannah Research Library and Municipal Archives, Savannah, GA.
38. Lizzie Boatright, Applications for Clemency, 001–04–042, Georgia Archives, Morrow, Georgia, hereafter cited as GA.
39. "Making an Investigation," *Morning News*, October 25, 1896.
40. "Added to Road Gang," *Marshall Messenger*, July 30, 1915; "Sends Woman to Chain Gang," *Des Moines Tribune*, August 8, 1911; "A Bad Daughter," *Mobile*

Daily Times, July 24, 1866; "Negro Women on Chain Gang in S.C.," *Weekly Review*, September 9, 1944.

41. "The City Court," *Clarion-Ledger*, August 7, 1897; "Calico Chain Gang," *Weekly Democrat*, September 1, 1897; "Simple Pathos," *Weekly Democrat-Times*, October 9, 1897.
42. "The City Court," *Clarion-Ledger*, August 7, 1897; "The Female Chain Gang," *Clarion-Ledger*, August 9, 1897.
43. "Arizona Sheriff Is First to Put Female Inmates on Chain Gang," *Macon Telegraph*, September 20, 1996.
44. Statistics show that Black Americans are twice as likely as whites to be stopped by the police, searched, arrested, and detained on cash bail or pretrial detention. These racial disparities are even more significant for Black women, who experience arrest rates nearly three times higher than white women and incarceration at an equally disproportionate level. For further reading, see "Policing Women: Race and Gender Disparities in Police Stops, Searches, and Use of Force," *Prison Policy Initiative*, May 14, 2019, https://www.prisonpolicy.org/blog/2019/05/14/policingwomen/, and Andrea J. Ritchie, *Invisible No More: Police Violence Against Black Women and Women of Color* (Boston: Beacon Press, 2017).
45. US Department of Justice, Civil Rights Division, "Investigation of the Ferguson Police Department," March 4, 2015, 62.
46. Brent Staples, "The Ferguson Nightmare," *New York Times*, March 5, 2015, https://archive.nytimes.com/takingnote.blogs.nytimes.com/2015/03/05/the-ferguson-nightmare/; US Department of Justice, Civil Rights Division, "Investigation of the Ferguson Police Department," 2.
47. US Department of Justice, Civil Rights Division, "Investigation of the Ferguson Police Department," 4.
48. "Single Moms Get Sucked into the Cruelest Debtors' Prison We've Ever Seen," ACLU Tennessee, December 21, 2018, https://www.aclu-tn.org/en/news/single-moms-get-sucked-cruelest-debtors-prison-weve-ever-seen.
49. Twyla Carter, "The Case Against Galveston County's Pretrial Detention System Survives the Government's Challenge," ACLU, January 18, 2019, https://www.aclu.org/news/racial-justice/case-against-galveston-countys-pretrial-detention.

CHAPTER 4: PROFITING PRISONS

1. "She Has Escaped: Nora Lay, Who Was Tried Just After Mrs. M'Kee," *Atlanta Constitution*, May 3, 1891. By definition, a determinate sentence is a prison sentence of a fixed length that cannot be reviewed or changed.
2. "A Negro with a Bad Record," *Morning News*, February 20, 1891.
3. "A Colored Girl Escapes," *Morning News*, May 3, 1891.
4. "Escaped Again: Nora Lay Gets Away a Second Time," *Atlanta Constitution*, May 29, 1891.
5. "So She Could Hang: Nora Lay Would Rather Hang Than Serve Ninety-Nine Years," *Atlanta Constitution*, May 6, 1891.

6. "Saints in Stripes," *Atlanta Journal*, May 18, 1891.
7. Various scholars of convict leasing argue that the prison system was the main provider of cheap labor in the post-Emancipation South. Readings that support this analysis include Mary Ellen Curtin, *Black Prisoners and Their World, Alabama, 1865–1900* (Charlottesville: University of Virginia Press, 2000); Alex Lichtenstein, *Twice the Work of Free Labor: The Political Economy of Convict Labor in the New South* (New York: Verso, 1996); LeFlouria, *Chained in Silence*; Matthew Mancini, *One Dies, Get Another: Convict Leasing in the American South, 1866–1928* (Columbia: University of South Carolina Press, 1996); Milfred C. Fierce, *Slavery Revisited: Blacks and the Southern Convict Lease System, 1865–1933* (New York: Africana Studies Center, 1994); Karin A. Shapiro, *A New South Rebellion: The Battle Against Convict Labor in the Tennessee Coalfields, 1871–1896* (Chapel Hill: University of North Carolina Press, 1998); Sarah Haley, *No Mercy Here: Gender, Punishment, and the Making of Jim Crow Modernity* (Chapel Hill: University of North Carolina Press, 2016); Robert Perkinson, *Texas Tough: The Rise of America's Prison Empire* (New York: Metropolitan Books, 2010); and Blackmon, *Slavery by Another Name*.
8. For a history of imprisoned white men's participation in the Civil War effort as Confederate soldiers and producers of wartime supplies, see Brett J. Derbes, "The Production of Military Supplies at the Alabama State Penitentiary During the Civil War," *Alabama Review* 67, no. 2 (April 2014): 131–60; and Brett J. Derbes, "Origins of the Prison Industrial Complex: Inmate Labor in the Deep South, 1817–1865," in *Reconsidering Southern Labor History: Race, Class, and Power*, ed. Matthew Hild and Keri Leigh Merritt (Gainesville: University Press of Florida, 2018).
9. "Locked Up: The Prison Labor That Built Business Empires," *Reveal* (podcast), September 17, 2022, https://revealnews.org/podcast/locked-up-the-prison-labor-that-built-business-empires/; Len Boselovic, "Steel Standing: U.S. Steel Celebrates 100 Years," *Pittsburgh Post-Gazette*, February 25, 2001, https://web.archive.org/web/20181012210047/http://old.post-gazette.com/businessnews/20010225ussteel2.asp. In *Slavery by Another Name*, Douglas A. Blackmon sheds new light on U.S. Steel and its involvement in convict leasing. His book is significant to our understanding of how the company derived its massive wealth through the exploitation of prison labor.
10. Curtin, *Black Prisoners and Their World*, 167.
11. Georgia, US, *Central Register of Convicts*, 1817–1976, Ancestry.com, Lehi, UT: Ancestry.com Operations Inc., 2014, https://www.ancestry.com; "Memorandum of Convicts Received by Penitentiary Co. No. 3, 1884," Registers of Convicts Received, Pardoned, Discharged, Died, or Escaped, 1871–86, RG 021–01–014, GA.
12. LeFlouria, *Chained in Silence*, 82; Blackmon, *Slavery by Another Name*, 343–45; David Charles Berry, "Free Labor He Found Unsatisfactory: James W. English and Convict Lease Labor at the Chattahoochee Brick Company" (master's thesis, Georgia State University, 1991), 35.

13. Corporal Punishment Monthly Reports (Whipping Reports), 1884–89, Georgia Department of Corrections, RG 21-1-11, GA.
14. "Saints in Stripes."
15. 1860 US Federal Census, slave schedules (Ancestry.com).
16. "A Queer Colony of Female Convicts," *Weekly News and Courier* (Charleston, SC), 1897.
17. "Table 2 Showing Rate of Injury, Sickness, and Death at Camp Heardmont by Number of Reported Cases, 1892–1897," in LeFlouria, *Chained in Silence*, 129–30.
18. Raymond E. Chandler Jr., "Death Comes to the Meanest Man in Georgia," *Georgia Backroads* 10, no. 2 (Summer 2011): 46. Bud Hilley relayed information about the murder of infants at Camp Heardmont to Raymond E. Chandler Sr., father of the author, during the 1930s.
19. "Women in Stripes," *Atlanta Constitution*, August 16, 1893.
20. "Women in Stripes."
21. "Women in Stripes."
22. The figure of the "mammy" is a racial stereotype that originates from slavery in the United States. This archetype embodies deference to white authority, with the mammy's primary role being to care for the needs of white families. The stereotype portrays Black women as idealized caregivers who are loyal, maternal, nonthreatening, and submissive.
23. "Women in Stripes."
24. The scholarship of Thavolia Glymph and Stephanie E. Jones-Rogers on plantation mistresses and the power they possessed has transformed our previous understanding of these women. Their research demonstrates that these women had authority within the plantation household and economy, and often demonstrated cruel acts of violence against enslaved people whom they owned and controlled. For further reading, see Thavolia Glymph, *Out of the House of Bondage: The Transformation of the Plantation Household* (Cambridge: Cambridge University Press, 2008); and Stephanie E. Jones-Rogers, *They Were Her Property: White Women as Slave Owners in the American South* (New Haven, CT: Yale University Press, 2019).
25. This figure comes from the 1850 US Federal Census, slave schedules, where Singleton Walthall Allen, Rebecca Mattox's father, is listed as the "slave owner" of 186 people. See 1850 US Federal Census, slave schedules, Ancestry.com, Lehi, UT: Ancestry.com Operations Inc., 2004, https://www.ancestry.com. When Allen died, he deeded his enslaved laborers to his wife, Jane Lanier Heard Allen. She is listed in the 1860 US Federal Census, slave schedules (Ancestry.com) as a "slave owner." During this year, she held possession of forty-four enslaved people.
26. "Return of the Exiles," *Daily Memphis Avalanche*, January 2, 1883. Fortune Dow, Pat. Gleason, Sam. McClelland, Pat Murray, Ben Wheeler, Stephen Ryan, John Weston, John Hennessey, Henry Thompson, John Redmond, Hugh Watts, Alex Dixon, Wesley Moore, Tun Wyley, George D. Powell, Tim Daley, Tom

Schafer, John Melville, Arthur Rollins, J. W. Cofer, Thad. Adkins, J. N. Gibson, A. Buford, Henry Cassel, Chauncey Williams, Jas. Sexton, A. Tanner, Sam. Cedarberg, Alex Hill, E. K. Ryan, Peter Lowrey, Dennis Carney, C. J. Jones, Len. Matthews, Bill Johnson, Maria Banks, Bill Lipsey, Willie Jones, William Macklin, Maria Avant, John Phillips, Annie Lewis, James Simonton, Mattie Taylor, James Holden, Mary Tate, John Kelley, Jerry Jackson, E. C. Knight, and Lizzie Johnson were among the persons redeemed from President's Island on this date. At the time of its expiration, Mary Forrest, Nathan Bedford Forrest's widow and his son, William Forrest, were in control of the family's convict lease farm on President's Island.

27. Frederic Bancroft, *Slave Trading in the Old South*, American Classics (New York: Frederick Ungar Publishing Co., 1959), 262–64; Jack Hurst, *Nathan Bedford Forrest: A Biography* (New York: A. A. Knopf, 1993), 58. Forrest's net income from slave trading is estimated to be $50,000 to $96,000.
28. "Ledger Lines," *Public Ledger*, July 8, 1875.
29. "List of Convicts at Work at General Forrest's," 1875, Prison Records, State of Tennessee, 1831–1992, Record Group 25-2-43, Tennessee State Library and Archives, Nashville, Tennessee.
30. "President's Island," *Public Ledger*, May 5, 1876.
31. "President's Island," *Daily Memphis Avalanche*," July 11, 1879. Grant's testimony was given to a newspaper after Nathan Bedford Forrest's death. The abuse he explains receiving may have occurred under the leadership of Mary Forrest, Forrest's widow, and his son, William Forrest. However, it appears that violence occurred throughout the duration of the plantation's existence.
32. "President's Island," *Daily Memphis Avalanche*.
33. "Local Paragraphs," *Memphis Daily Appeal*, February 21, 1877; "News in Brief," *Memphis Avalanche*, August 24, 1876.
34. "News in Brief." Misdemeanor convict leasing is a largely understudied topic. For a detailed history of this practice, see Thomas Aiello, *Bound Labor in the Turpentine Belt: Kinderlou Camp and Misdemeanor Convict Leasing in Georgia* (Gainesville: University Press of Florida, 2024).
35. "Ledger Lines," Public Ledger, January 5, 1877.
36. Letter from N. B. Forrest to Hon. Tom Holman, Chairman, County Court, Memphis, Tennessee, published in "The County Court," *Memphis Daily Appeal*, January 5, 1877.
37. "Ledger Lines," *Public Ledger*, October 20, 1875.
38. "The Hell Miniature," *Daily Memphis Avalanche*," July 16, 1880.
39. "Fire on President's Island," *Public Ledger*, December 6, 1877.
40. "Memphis," *The Tennessean*, January 12, 1878; "News in Brief," *Daily Memphis Avalanche*, January 13, 1880; "Sending Prisoners to the Island," *Daily Memphis Avalanche*, August 10, 1880.
41. "Penitentiary Birds," *Memphis Daily Appeal*, May 22, 1878. A grand jury report from July 1878 documented 125 prisoners on President's Island at the time of the women's confinement: one hundred Black males, nine Black females, fifteen

white males, and one white female. "Grand Jury's Report," *Public Ledger*, July 11, 1878.

42. "The Dollar Weekly Avalanche," *Daily Memphis Avalanche*, May 10, 1878.
43. "Damage Suits," *Memphis Daily Appeal*, August 10, 1880.
44. Mary Church Terrell, "Peonage in the United States: The Convict Lease System and the Chain Gangs," *Nineteenth Century* 62 (July–December 1907): 308.
45. LeFlouria, *Chained in Silence*, 157.
46. E. C. Bruffey, "State Farm Conditions That Foster Injustice," *Atlanta Constitution*, August 16, 1903.
47. "I Refused Warden's Advances, Told of Them, and He Lashed Me," *Atlanta Constitution*, August 12, 1903.
48. "I Refused Warden's Advances, Told of Them, and He Lashed Me."
49. John Avery Lomax and unidentified group of Black women prisoners, *Waitin' on You*, Georgia State Prison Farm, Milledgeville, GA, 1934, AFS 00262 A01, and John Avery Lomax and unidentified group of Black women prisoners, *Beautiful Gate*, Georgia State Prison Farm, Milledgeville, GA, 1934, AFS 00262 A02, American Folklife Center, Library of Congress, Washington, DC. For further reading on the history of Black women's incarceration on state prison farms, see David M. Oshinsky, *Worse Than Slavery: Parchman Farm and the Ordeal of Jim Crow Justice* (New York: Free Press, 1996); Vivien M. L. Miller, *Hard Labor and Hard Time: Florida's "Sunshine Prison" and Chain Gangs* (Gainesville: University Press of Florida, 2012); Telisha Dionne Bailey, "'Please Don't Forget About Me': African American Women, Mississippi, and the History of Crime and Punishment in Parchman Prison, 1890–1980" (PhD diss., University of Mississippi, 2015); Nathalie Rech, "Locking Up and Exploiting African American Women at Angola State Penitentiary: Experiences of Incarceration in Jim Crow Louisiana (1901–1961)" (PhD diss., Université du Québec à Montréal, 2022); and Jane Howe Gregory, "Persistence and Irony in the Incarceration of Women in the Texas Penitentiary, 1907–1910" (master's thesis, Rice University, 1994).
50. The author acknowledges that racial disparities have long existed in the history of Black women's incarceration, and that these disparities have not been exclusively confined to the South. Even in parts of the North and Midwest where Black women made up a very small percentage of the female population, they were overrepresented in the prison system. These trends persisted throughout chattel slavery and in the decades following the Civil War.
51. Aleks Kajstura and Wendy Sawyer, *Women's Mass Incarceration: The Whole Pie 2024*, Northampton, MA, Prison Policy Initiative, March 5, 2024, https://www.prisonpolicy.org/reports/pie2024women.html.
52. Kali Nicole Gross, "African American Women, Mass Incarceration, and the Politics of Protection," *Journal of American History* 102, no. 1 (June 2015): 29. On the War on Drugs and its impact on Black women, see Stephanie R. Bush-Baskette, "The War on Drugs as a War Against Black Women," in *Crime Control and Women: Feminist Implications of Criminal Justice Policy*, ed. Susan Miller

(Thousand Oaks, CA: SAGE Publications, 1998), 113–29; Stephanie R. Bush-Baskette, *Misguided Justice: The War on Drugs and the Incarceration of Black Women* (Bloomington, IN: iUniverse, 2010); Susan Burton and Cari Lynn, *Becoming Ms. Burton: From Prison to Recovery to Leading the Fight for Incarcerated Women* (New York: New Press, 2017); and Kemba Smith, *Poster Child: The Kemba Smith Story* (Richmond, VA: IBJ Book Publishing, 2011). See also Trevariana Mason, *Extreme Sentences Disproportionately Impact and Harm Black Women*, National Black Women's Justice Institute, September 23, 2021, https://www.nbwji.org/post/extreme-sentences-disproportionately-impact-and-harm-black-women, and Samuel L. Myers Jr., William J. Sabol, and Man Xu, *The Determinants of Declining Racial Disparities in Female Incarceration Rates, 2000–2015*, Prison Policy Initiative, December 31, 2018, https://www.prisonpolicy.org/scans/thedeterminantsofdecliningracialdisparities.pdf.

53. Only 4 percent of the world's female population resides in the United States, yet the country accounts for over 30 percent of the world's incarcerated women. For further reading, see Aleks Kajstura, *States of Women's Incarceration: The Global Context 2018*, Prison Policy Initiative, June 2018, https://www.prisonpolicy.org/global/women/2018.html.
54. For access to the full letter, see "CCA Letter," *Huffington Post*, https://big.assets.huffingtonpost.com/ccaletter.pdf.
55. Financial figures for CoreCivic and GEO Group are drawn from the following sources: CoreCivic, Inc., *CoreCivic Reports Fourth Quarter and Full Year 2024 Financial Results*, Brentwood, TN, February 10, 2025, https://ir.corecivic.com/node/24301/pdf; CoreCivic, Inc., *2024 Annual Report*, Brentwood, TN, 2025, https://ir.corecivic.com/static-files/e3725fbb-67d7–49fc-b0b9-ed30e70e47cf; The GEO Group, Inc., *The GEO Group Reports Fourth Quarter and Full Year 2024 Results*, Boca Raton, FL, February 27, 2025, https://investors.geogroup.com/node/18081/pdf; and the GEO Group, Inc., *2024 Annual Report*, Boca Raton, FL, 2025, https://investors.geogroup.com/static-files/0e302371–9812–435b-8560-bfe62d4949da.
56. Kristen M. Budd, *Private Prisons in the United States*, The Sentencing Project, February 21, 2024, https://www.sentencingproject.org/reports/private-prisons-in-the-united-states/.
57. L. B. Wright, "The American Prison System: It's Just Business," *Journal of Civil Rights and Economic Development*, December 9, 2018, https://news.law.fordham.edu/jcfl/2018/12/09/the-american-prison-system-its-just-business/. For readings on the contemporary for-profit prison industry, see Bianca Tylek, *The Prison Industry: How It Works and Who Profits* (New York: The New Press, 2025); Tara Herivel and Paul Wright, eds., *Prison Profiteers: Who Makes Money from Mass Incarceration* (New York: The New Press, 2009); Donna Selman and Paul Leighton, *Punishment for Sale: Private Prisons, Big Business, and the Incarceration Binge* (Lanham, MD: Rowman & Littlefield Publishers, 2010); and Lauren-Brooke Eisen, *Inside Private Prisons: An American Dilemma in the Age of Mass Incarceration* (New York: Columbia University Press, 2019).

58. Business & Human Rights Resource Centre, "USA: More than 500 Businesses Including McDonald's, Burger King and Walmart Using Alabama Prisoners as Cheap Labour, a Two-Year Investigation Has Found," August 18, 2023, https://www.business-humanrights.org/en/latest-news/usa-more-than-500-businesses-including-mcdonalds-burger-king-and-walmart-using-alabama-prisoners-as-cheap-labour-a-two-year-investigation-has-found/; Corporate Accountability Lab, "Private Companies Producing with U.S. Prison Labor in 2020 (Prison Labor in the U.S., Part II)," August 5, 2020, https://corpaccountabilitylab.org/calblog/2020/8/5/private-companies-producing-with-us-prison-labor-in-2020-prison-labor-in-the-us-part-ii; Malta Justice Initiative, "12 Major Corporations Benefiting from the Prison Industrial Complex," 2024, https://maltajusticeinitiative.org/12-major-corporations-benefiting-from-the-prison-industrial-complex-2/; and Shane Bauer, "Your Family's Genealogical Records May Have Been Digitized by a Prisoner," *Mother Jones*, August 13, 2015, https://www.motherjones.com/politics/2015/08/mormon-church-prison-geneology-family-search/.
59. Nina Mast, "Rooted in Racism: An Analysis of Prison Labor," Economic Policy Institute, September 13, 2022, https://www.epi.org/publication/rooted-racism-prison-labor/. Information on the current compensation rate for incarcerated workers comes from Wendy Sawyer and Peter Wagner, *Mass Incarceration: The Whole Pie 2025*, Prison Policy Initiative, March 11, 2025, https://www.prisonpolicy.org/reports/pie2025.html.
60. For a comprehensive, economic analysis of mass incarceration's devastating impact on Black communities, see Tasseli McKay, *Stolen Wealth, Hidden Power: The Case for Reparations for Mass Incarceration* (Oakland: University of California Press, 2022).

CHAPTER 5: FAMILY SEPARATION

1. Testimony of Stephanie J., collected November 18, 2021, Black Women and Mass Incarceration Archive, private collection belonging to Dr. Talitha L. LeFlouria, hereafter cited as BWMI Archive. To maintain the anonymity of the individual giving testimony, I have chosen not to disclose her last name or town of residence.
2. Bethany Veney, *The Narrative of Bethany Veney: A Slave Woman* (1889), 26, Documenting the American South, https://docsouth.unc.edu/fpn/veney/veney.html.
3. Christopher A. Swann and Michelle Sheran Sylvester, "The Foster Care Crisis: What Caused Caseloads to Grow?" *Demography* 43, no. 2 (May 2006): 309–35; US Department of Health and Human Services, Administration for Children and Families, Children's Bureau, *The AFCARS Report: Final Estimates for FY 1998 Through FY 2002 (12)* (October 2006), https://acf.gov/sites/default/files/documents/cb/afcarsreport12.pdf. (AFCARS stands for Adoption and Foster Care Analysis and Reporting System.)
4. US Department of Health and Human Services, Administration for Children and Families, Children's Bureau, *ACYF-CB-PI-15–08: Adoption and Legal*

Guardianship Incentive Payments (Washington, DC, July 8, 2015), https://acf.gov/sites/default/files/documents/cb/pi1508.pdf; Mary Eschelbach Hansen, "State-Designated Special Needs, Post-Adoption Support, and State Fiscal Stress," *Child and Youth Services Review* 29, no. 11 (November 2007): 1413.

5. US Department of Health and Human Services, Administration for Children and Families, Children's Bureau, *Adoption and Legal Guardianship Incentive Payment Program: Earning History by State: FY 1998–FY 2023* (Washington, DC, September 2024), https://acf.gov/sites/default/files/documents/cb/algipp-earning-history-by-state_0.pdf; "Trends in Foster Care and Adoption: FY 2013-2022," AFCARS data, US Children's Bureau, Administration for Children, Youth, and Families, March 20, 2024, https://acf.gov/cb/report/trends-foster-care-adoption. Historian Melissa DeVelvis estimates that fifty thousand Black children were sold through the domestic slave trade. For further reading, see Melissa DeVelvis, "Enslaved Children, Trauma, and 'American Family Values': A Recap of the 2021 Southern's SAWH Keynote," in *Muster: How the Past Informs the Present* (blog of the *Journal of the Civil War Era*), December 21, 2021, https://www.journalofthecivilwarera.org/2021/12/enslaved-children-trauma-and-american-family-values-a-recap-of-the-2021-southerns-sawh-keynote. In 1998, one year after the Adoption and Safe Families Act was ratified and during the peak of the War on Drugs, approximately 229,000 Black children were placed in foster care. Although the exact number of Black children adopted that year is not documented, it is estimated that of a total 37,000 adoptions, around 15,170 were Black. This estimate is based on the fact that in 1998, 41 percent of the children in the child welfare system were of African descent.
6. Henry Box Brown, *Narrative of the Life of Henry Box Brown, Written by Himself* (1851), 2, Documenting the American South, https://docsouth.unc.edu/neh/brownbox/brownbox.html.
7. Brown, *Narrative of the Life of Henry Box Brown*, 40–41.
8. Brown, *Narrative of the Life of Henry Box Brown*, 46.
9. Michael Tadman, "Slave Trading in the Ante-Bellum South: An Estimate of the Extent of the Inter-Regional Slave Trade," *Journal of American Studies* 13, no. 2 (August 1979): 196. Although the domestic slave trade was a major cause of family separation, there were other circumstances that led to families being torn apart, including being sold to settle an enslaver's debts, individual sales ordered by the courts, being given away as gifts or inheritances, being sold by a jail to repay jail fees, or being sold as a form of punishment.
10. For further reading on the story of Ashley's sack, see Tiya Miles, *All That She Carried: The Journey of Ashley's Sack, A Black Family Keepsake* (New York: Random House, 2022), and Mark Auslander, "Slavery's Traces: In Search of Ashley's Sack," *Southern Spaces* (November 29, 2016), https://southernspaces.org/2016/slaverystraces-search-ashleys-sack/.
11. Register of Slave Commitments to the DC Jail, 1848–1862, accession no. DCA 97–01, DCPR. "Laura + two children" appear in the ledger for the year 1856. Given Washington, DC's role as a supplier for the domestic slave trade, it is

possible that Laura and her children were sold to the Deep South for a price much higher than the cost of their jail fees.

12. Jennifer L. Morgan, "Partus sequitur ventrem: Law, Race, and Reproduction in Colonial Slavery," *Small Axe* 22, no. 1 (March 2018), no. 55: 1.
13. For further reading on the history of apprenticeship for free Black children, see Millward, *Finding Charity's Folk*. See also Mary Frances Berry, *Slavery After Slavery: Revealing the Legacy of Forced Child Apprenticeships on Black Families, from Emancipation to the Present* (Boston: Beacon Press, 2025).
14. Theodore Brantner Wilson, *The Black Codes of the South* (Tuscaloosa: University of Alabama Press, 1965), 39.
15. Clement Dorsey, *The General Public Statutory Law and Public Local Law of the State of Maryland: From the Year 1692 to 1839 Inclusive, with Annotations Thereto, and a Copious Index* (Baltimore: John D. Toy, 1840), 697, Archives of Maryland Online, https://msa.maryland.gov/megafile/msa/speccol/sc2900/sc2908/000001/000141/html/am141--697.html.
16. Dorsey, *General Public Statutory Law*, 562, https://msa.maryland.gov/megafile/msa/speccol/sc2900/sc2908/000001/000141/html/am141--562.html https://msa.maryland.gov/megafile/msa/speccol/sc2900/sc2908/000001/000141/html/am141--561.html; https://msa.maryland.gov/megafile/msa/speccol/sc2900/sc2908/000001/000141/html/am141--562.html.
17. Schweninger Collection, MSA SC 4239, M 11020, MSA. Petition filed by James Wilson to sell the unexpired term of Augusta Spriggs's apprenticeship, filed December 2, 1856, in *Race, Slavery, and Free Blacks: Petitions to Southern County Courts, Series II, Maryland, 1856*. Accessed in ProQuest History Vault; petition filed by David H. White to sell the unexpired term of Augusta Spriggs's apprenticeship, filed July 26, 1854, in *Race, Slavery, and Free Blacks: Petitions to Southern County Courts, Series II, Maryland, 1856*. Accessed in ProQuest History Vault, https://www.proquest.com/hvslaveryandlaw/results/A88059E455C4405FPQ/1?accountid=7118.
18. "Advertisement," *The Sun*, November 27, 1856.
19. Dorsey, *General Public Statutory Law*, 508, https://msa.maryland.gov/megafile/msa/speccol/sc2900/sc2908/000001/000388/html/am388--508.html.
20. 1850 US Federal Census, slave schedules (Ancestry.com); 1860 US Federal Census, slave schedules (Ancestry.com).
21. "Advertisement," *The Sun*, April 4, 1857.
22. Dorsey, *General Public Statutory Law*, 629. https://msa.maryland.gov/megafile/msa/speccol/sc2900/sc2908/000001/000141/html/am141--629.html.
23. Vernetta D. Young, "All the Women in the Maryland State Penitentiary: 1812–1869," *Prison Journal* 81, no. 1 (March 2001): 117.
24. Last Seen: Finding Family After Slavery, Villanova University, https://informationwanted.org; Judith Giesberg, *Last Seen: The Enduring Search by Formerly Enslaved People to Find Their Lost Families* (New York: Simon & Schuster, 2025). For a comprehensive history of formerly enslaved people's search for lost family members, see Heather A. Williams, *Help Me to Find My People: The African*

American Search for Family Lost in Slavery (Chapel Hill: University of North Carolina Press, 2016).

25. "Mattie Searching for Her Daughter, Emma," *New York Age*, January 24, 1907, Last Seen: Finding Family After Slavery, https://informationwanted.org/items/show/5233.
26. "Joe Slatton Searching for His Mother, Rosie Ingram," *National Baptist Union-Review* (Nashville, TN), December 25, 1909, Last Seen: Finding Family After Slavery, https://informationwanted.org/items/show/5382.
27. "'Uncle Levi' and 'Aunt Aggie' Reunited and Remarried After 40 Years," *Butler (MO) Weekly Times*, January 30, 1884, Last Seen: Finding Family After Slavery, https://informationwanted.org/items/show/3290.
28. It is important to mention that, in the historical record, there are rare exceptions where Black parents voluntarily apprenticed their children. However, these arrangements were usually always involuntary for Black children, even when they "consented" to be hired out. The power imbalance between Black children and the adults negotiating their labor did not allow them a choice.
29. Aima Ship to Leathe, May 13, 1866, and Aima Ship to Adeline, May 13, 1866, in Col. J. R. Lewis to Bvt. Maj. C. B. Fisk, June 29, 1866, L-84 1866, Registered Letters Received, series 3379, Tennessee Assistant Commissioner, Bureau of Refugees, Freedmen, and Abandoned Lands, Record Group 105, National Archives and Records Administration; Freedmen and Southern Society Project, https://www.freedmen.umd.edu/Ship.html.
30. Records of the Assistant Commissioner for the District of Columbia, Bureau of Refugees, Freedmen and Abandoned Lands, 1865–1869, National Archives Microfilm Publication M1055, roll 21, "Miscellaneous Reports and Lists"; the Freedmen's Bureau Online, Records of the Bureau of Refugees, Freedmen and Abandoned Lands, https://freedmensbureau.com/washingtondc/outrages.htm.
31. The Freedmen's Bureau Online, https://freedmensbureau.com/washingtondc/outrages.htm.
32. Samuel Coston v. Leah Coston, Mother and Next Friend of Simon Coston and Washington Coston, writ of error to the Criminal Court of Baltimore City, no. 115, General Docket, Court of Appeals of Maryland, October term, 1865, https://msa.maryland.gov/megafile/msa/speccol/sc5300/sc5339/000257/000000/000014/restricted/msa_sc5458_51_5006_5.pdf; Samuel S. Coston v. Leah Coston, Court of Appeals of Maryland, decided July 17, 1866, https://msa.maryland.gov/megafile/msa/speccol/sc5300/sc5339/000257/000000/000014/restricted/25_md_500.pdf.
33. Richard Paul Fuke, *Imperfect Equality: African Americans and the Confines of White Racial Attitudes in Post-Emancipation Maryland* (New York: Fordham University Press, 1999), 83.
34. Unfortunately, when Black parents did not show up to court or failed to prove their parental worthiness, judges often gave their children to white individuals whom they deemed more equipped to raise them.
35. "General News," *New York Times*, July 16, 1865.

36. The comments of Mary and John Morst's great-granddaughter Kimberlea appear in the following blog post: UncommonWealth: Voices from the Library of Virginia (blog), "Mug Shot Monday: Mary L. Morst, No. 11033," December 19, 2011, https://uncommonwealth.virginiamemory.com/blog/2011/12/19/mug-shot-monday-mary-l-morst-no-11033/.
37. Letter from Mary Morst to Superintendent J. B. Wood, January 5, 1915, Records of the Virginia Penitentiary, Series IV, Office of the Superintendent, Subseries B, General Correspondence, Superintendent J. B. Wood, box 402, folder 6, accession 41558, Library of Virginia, Richmond, VA, hereafter cited as LVA; UncommonWealth: Voices from the Library of Virginia (blog), "Mug Shot Monday: Mary L. Morst, No. 11033," December 19, 2011, https://uncommonwealth.virginiamemory.com/blog/2011/12/19/mug-shot-monday-mary-l-morst-no-11033/.
38. Letter from Kate A. Plecker to Governor Westmoreland Davis, February 21, 1921, Mary L. Morst Pardon File, box 569, LVA; "Mug Shot Monday: Mary L. Morst, No. 11033," UncommonWealth: Voices from the Library of Virginia (blog), December 19, 2011, https://uncommonwealth.virginiamemory.com/blog/2011/12/19/mug-shot-monday-mary-l-morst-no-11033/.
39. 1930 US Federal Census, Ancestry.Com, Lehi, UT: Ancestry.com Operations Inc., 2002, https://www.ancestry.com.
40. Letter from Ella Gamble to Joseph S. Turner, July 31, 1904. Ella Gamble, Applications for Clemency, 001–04–042, GA.
41. "Sentenced for Life," *Norfolk Virginian*, October 25, 1884.
42. Georgia, Central Register of Convicts, 1817–1976 (Ancestry.com).
43. "Saints in Stripes."
44. Letter from Ella Gamble to Joseph S. Turner, July 7, 1904. Ella Gamble, Applications for Clemency, GA.
45. 1900 US Federal Census, Ancestry.com, Lehi, UT: Ancestry.com Operations Inc., 2004, https://www.ancestry.com.
46. As of September 2024, the US government paid $1,003,288,375 into the Adoption and Legal Guardianship Incentive Payment Program. For a detailed report of the program's earning history by state from 1998 to 2024, see US Department of Health and Human Services, Administration for Children and Families, *Adoption and Legal Guardianship Incentive Payments, Earning History by State, 1998–2024*, September 2024, https://acf.gov/sites/default/files/documents/cb/algipp-earning-history-by-state_0.pdf. See also Elizabeth Brico, "The Government Spends 10 Times More on Foster Care and Adoption Than Reuniting Families," TalkPoverty.org, Center for American Progress, August 23, 2019. Although the Adoption and Safe Families Act (ASFA) greatly encourages adoption through financial incentives and policy changes, it was built upon earlier legislation that had already provided financial support for adoption, especially for children with disabilities. The Adoption Assistance and Child Welfare Act of 1980 (AACWA) established the first federal incentives specifically aimed at families adopting children with "special needs."

47. For more information about the Bureau of Land Management's Adoption Incentive Program, see US Bureau of Land Management, "Celebrating Five Years: Adoption Incentive Program a Win-Win for Animals and Taxpayers," Bureau of Land Management (blog), May 22, 2024, https://www.blm.gov/blog/2024-05-22/celebrating-five-years-adoption-incentive-program-win-win-animals-and-taxpayers. Details about complaints and the court ruling suspending the program, see "Adoption Incentive Program," Skydog Ranch, https://www.skydogranch.org/adoption-incentive-program, and Dave Philipps, "Wild Horses Adopted Under a Federal Program Are Going to Slaughter," *New York Times*, May 15, 2021, https://www.nytimes.com/2021/05/15/us/wild-horses-adoptions-slaughter.html.
48. Dorothy Roberts coined the term "family policing system" to describe how state-controlled systems of child "welfare" function to surveil and control Black families. For further reading, see Dorothy Roberts, *Torn Apart: How the Child Welfare System Destroys Black Families—and How Abolition Can Build a Safer World* (New York: Basic Books, 2022).
49. Testimony of Myesha Johnson, collected December 18, 2021, BWMI Archive.
50. Testimony of Kyndia Riley, collected July 25, 2022, BWMI Archive.

CHAPTER 6: TRACKING FREEDOM

1. Mattie Lee Reid, Applications for Clemency, 001–04–042, GA.
2. Mattie Lee Reid, Applications for Clemency.
3. Mattie Lee Reid, Applications for Clemency.
4. Mattie Lee Reid, Applications for Clemency.
5. There are few financial records that document these payments. Nevertheless, there is significant evidence of city and state ordinances requiring securities from guardians. For example, in the city of Macon, Georgia, guardians were required to "give a bond and approved security in the sum of four hundred dollars for the good conduct of said free person of color or slave." It is assumed that free people repaid these fees through leveraging their assets, making monetary payments, or through their labor. See "Ordinances for the Internal Government of the Town of Macon," passed by the Board of Commissioners, March 1829, printed in *Macon Telegraph*, April 4, 1829. For further reading on the guardianship system as it operated in Georgia, see Janice L. Sumler-Edmond, "Free Black Life in Savannah," in *Slavery and Freedom in Savannah*, Leslie M. Harris and Daina Ramey Berry (Athens: University of Georgia Press, 2014), and Ralph B. Flanders, "The Free Negro in Ante-bellum Georgia," *North Carolina Historical Review* 9, no. 3 (July 1932): 250–72. On guardianship in various antebellum Southern states, see Jasmine E. Harris, "The Political Economy of Conservatorship," *UCLA Law Review* 71 (2024): 1364–1482.
6. Sumler-Edmond, "Free Black Life in Savannah," 135–36.
7. "Eliza Saturday [Curtis], a Free Person of Color, Seeks the Appointment of Bryant Wasden as a Guardian for Her, Her Property, and Her Two Children, William and Frank," 1842, in *Race, Slavery, and Free Blacks: Petitions to Southern County*

Courts, Series II, Georgia. Accessed in ProQuest History Vault, https://www.proquest.com/hvslaveryandlaw/docview/2634664601/2B68EF2A3F8543E2PQ/1?accountid=7118&sourcetype=Archival%20Materials.

8. "Nancy Coleman, a Free Person of Color, States That Thomas Barnes Has Served as the Guardian for Herself and Her Children, But He Has Died. Coleman Asks the Court to Appoint Peter Scott as Their New Guardian. Nancy Coleman's Children Are Named Mary, Thomas, Baker, and Jincy," 1836, in *Race, Slavery, and Free Blacks: Petitions to Southern County Courts, Series II, Georgia*. Accessed in ProQuest History Vault, https://www.proquest.com/hvslaveryandlaw/docview/2634664592/B774569037A946EEPQ/1?accountid=7118&sourcetype=Archival%20Materials; "Patsey King, a Free Woman of Color, States That She 'Is Exposed to All the Pains and Penalties, Enacted Against Free Persons of Color, Having No Guardian in This State.' She Seeks the Appointment of William H. Kistler as Her Guardian," 1853, in *Race, Slavery, and Free Blacks: Petitions to Southern County Courts, Series II, Georgia*. Accessed in ProQuest History Vault, https://www.proquest.com/hvslaveryandlaw/docview/2634671337/DC83950753604I2EPQ/1?accountid=7118&sourcetype=Archival%20Materials.
9. "Freedmen's Bureau," *Encyclopedia of Race and Racism*, Encyclopedia.com, https://www.encyclopedia.com/social-sciences/encyclopedias-almanacs-transcripts-and-maps/freedmens-bureau.
10. For a detailed study of the Freedmen's Bureau's treatment of Black women and its approach to the "vagrancy problem" after 1865, see Mary Farmer-Kaiser, "'Are They Not in Some Sorts Vagrants?': Gender and the Efforts of the Freedmen's Bureau to Combat Vagrancy in the Reconstruction South," *Georgia Historical Quarterly* 88, no. 1 (Spring 2004): 25–49, and Mary Farmer-Kaiser, *Freedwomen and the Freedmen's Bureau*.
11. Texas State Library and Archives Commission, *Convict Record Ledgers*, B 04021–052020, vol. 1998/038–16, Department of Criminal Justice, Archives and Information Services Division, Texas State Library and Archives Commission, Austin, Texas, hereafter cited as TSLAC.
12. Jermaine Thibodeaux, "The House That Cane Built: Sugar, Race, and the Gendered Foundations of the Texas Prison System," 1843–1920 (PhD diss., The University of Texas at Austin, 2021), 137.
13. Paul Lucko, "Board of Pardons and Paroles," Texas State Historical Association, Handbook of Texas Online, published 1952, updated April 16, 2019, https://www.tshaonline.org/handbook/entries/board-of-pardons-and-paroles; Texas Department of Criminal Justice, "Parole Division: The History of Parole in Texas," https://www.tdcj.texas.gov/divisions/pd/history.html.
14. Escape Record Card, Anna Bell Johnson, issued December 23, 1926, Texas Prison Museum Archive, Huntsville, Texas.
15. Texas State Library and Archives Commission, *Conduct Registers*, vols. 1998/038–177–1998/038–236, Texas Department of Criminal Justice, Archives and Information Services Division, TSLAC.

16. Geoffrey Birt, "Prison Chief Boswell for the Defense," July 31, 1949, *Montgomery Advertiser*. For reference to the 1940 Alabama Code, see "Boswell's Yule Paroles Draw Board Attack," *Birmingham News*, May 27, 1948.
17. "Convicts Used as Servants," *Alabama Journal*, December 4, 1948; "Convicts in Alabama Serve as Personal Servants," *Birmingham News*, December 12, 1948. In "Convicts in Alabama Serve as Personal Servants," there are numerous examples of Black male prisoners also being forced to provide uncompensated labor for prison officials and of these officials expensing the costs associated with the use of their labor to the state.
18. For a comprehensive history of the Julia Tutwiler Prison, see Tim Dodge, "Good Intentions, Disappointing Results: A History of the Julia Tutwiler Prison for Women," *Alabama Review* 61, no. 4 (October 2008): 243–303.
19. Curtin, *Black Prisoners and Their World*, 120.
20. "Convicts in Alabama Serve as Personal Servants," *Birmingham News*, 1948.
21. H. C. Flowers to J. F. Sewell, February 29, 1944, Department of Corrections and Institutions Administrative Correspondence, Julia Tutwiler and Draper Prison Physician Correspondence October 1943–August 1944, Alabama Department of Archives and History, as cited in Mary Dixie Dysart, "'No Place for a Christian': Women Inmates in Alabama Prisons, 1901–1943" (PhD diss., Auburn University, 1999), 245.
22. Geoffrey Birt, "Boswell Too Busy to List Convicts Used by Friends," *Alabama Journal*, December 9, 1948.
23. Trena Easley Armstrong, "The Hidden Help: Black Domestic Workers in the Civil Rights Movement" (master's thesis, University of Louisville, 2012), iv.
24. For readings on the history of Black women and domestic parole, see Cheryl D. Hicks, *Talk with You Like a Woman: African American Women, Justice, and Reform in New York, 1890–1935* (Chapel Hill: University of North Carolina Press, 2010) and Sarah Haley, *No Mercy Here: Gender, Punishment, and the Making of Jim Crow Modernity* (Chapel Hill: University of North Carolina Press, 2016). On paroled Black girls, see Lindsey E. Jones, "'The Most Unprotected of All Human Beings': Black Girls, State Violence, and the Limits of Protection in Jim Crow Virginia," *Souls: A Critical Journal of Black Politics, Culture, and Society* 20, no. 1 (December 2018): 1–25. Although the experiences of incarcerated Black girls are not discussed in *Searching for Jane Crow*, the author acknowledges the importance of their stories and encourages future scholars to research this understudied topic.
25. President Carter had himself designated as Mary Prince's parole officer, which enabled her to live and work at the White House during the term of his presidency. This fact is referenced in Kate Andersen Brower, *The Residence: Inside the Private World of the White House* (New York: HarperCollins, 2015), 186. Mary Prince's story is also covered in Sarah Haley, "Care Cage: Black Women, Political Symbolism, and 1970s Prison Crisis," *Souls* 20, no. 1 (January 2018): 58–85. Haley's article is the first scholarly work on the subject.

26. Gross, "African American Women, Mass Incarceration, and the Politics of Protection," 29.
27. Clare Crawford-Mason, "A Story of Love and Rehabilitation: The Ex-Con in the White House," *People*, March 14, 1977, https://web.archive.org/web/20150623232438/http://www.people.com/people/archive/article/0,,20067515,00.html.
28. Hillary Rodham Clinton, *It Takes a Village: And Other Lessons Children Teach Us* (New York: Simon & Schuster, 1996), 52.
29. Clinton, *It Takes a Village*, 52.
30. Crawford-Mason, "A Story of Love and Rehabilitation."
31. Brower, *The Residence*, 188.
32. Brower, *The Residence*.
33. Human Rights Watch, *Profiting from Probation: America's "Offender Funded" Probation Industry*, Human Rights Watch, February 5, 2014, https://www.hrw.org/report/2014/02/05/profiting-probation/americas-offender-funded-probation-industry.
34. "Probation and Parole Driving Mass Incarceration," Equal Justice Initiative, November 25, 2020, https://eji.org/news/probation-and-parole-driving-mass-incarceration/.

INDEX

ABOUT THE AUTHOR

Talitha L. LeFlouria is an associate professor of history and the Mastin Gentry White Fellow in Southern History at The University of Texas at Austin. She is the author of *Chained in Silence: Black Women and Convict Labor in the New South* (University of North Carolina Press, 2015), which won awards from the Organization of American Historians, the Association of Black Women Historians, the Berkshire Conference of Women Historians, and the Charles H. Wright Museum of African American History, among others.

Dr. LeFlouria received her PhD in US history from Howard University in Washington, DC, and has held positions with the Moorland-Spingarn Research Center in Washington, DC, the Frederick Douglass National Historic Site (National Park Service), Florida Atlantic University, and the University of Virginia. She is one of the nation's leading authorities on the history of Black women, mass incarceration, and the legacies of American slavery. She has made guest appearances on NPR and C-SPAN, and in documentaries including *One Thousand Years of Slavery*, produced by Angela Bassett and Courtney Vance for the Smithsonian Channel. Her work has been featured in the *Washington Post*, *The Atlantic*, *Vox*, *The Root*, and *Ms.*, and she has received several awards for her research, including an Andrew Carnegie Fellowship. *Searching for Jane Crow: Black Women and Mass Incarceration in America from the Auction Block to the Cell Block* is her second single-authored book.